Teacher's G

Yellow Umbrella Books—Early Level

Table of Contents

Guided Reading
AND
Yellow Umbrella Books

Understanding the Early Beginning Reader

Children who have mastered texts at the emergent level are still developing as readers but are ready for the next step; they are early readers. As children progress from emergent readers to early readers, they have gained a firm grasp of letters and many letter sounds. They can recognize basic punctuation marks and understand their functions, as well as the concept of a sentence. They are familiar with print, and they know to track print from left to right. The early reader is ready to move from books with predictable language to texts with more varied sentence structures and vocabularies. However, early readers are still far from being independent readers. They still need guidance and instruction, which makes small guided-reading groups the perfect way to continue developing children's reading abilities.

Guided Reading and Content-Rich Topics

Within the context of guided reading, small groups of children use similar reading strategies and processes, while teachers observe children as they read and provide supports that eventually facilitate independent reading. The teacher introduces the book, models reading strategies during a group read, and provides prompts that help children build background knowledge. These teaching strategies enable children to see reading as a meaning-making process that they can control. The goal of a guided-reading program is for young readers to learn to use what they know, make predictions, sample text, and check that what they read makes sense, sounds right, and looks right.

In a guided-reading program, running records and teacher observations are used to group children with similar instructional needs. Guided-reading groups are dynamic. Groupings can and should change as children grow and change in their reading behaviors and literacy learning. In this way, teachers can address individual children's needs, firm up children's known strategies, and move them from known concepts to new ones. Observing children as they read and acknowledging the texts with which they are familiar are fundamental to a guided-reading program. This "teacher knowledge" helps the teacher to select level-appropriate books, guide book introductions and lessons, and focus on appropriate teaching points to reinforce text features.

Often when we introduce books to young children we forget that they should not have to handle more than a few new ideas or skills as they read a new book. Children's familiarity with text content, language, and format become primary considerations when selecting content-based texts that both support and challenge early readers.

Within guided-reading groups, teachers can model for children effective reading strategies. Teachers can show children how to preview nonfiction texts, how to ask open-ended questions, and how to use a variety of strategies to solve problems. In order to make key concepts in the text more accessible, teachers can also introduce graphic organizers, such as two-column comparison charts, word webs, and Venn diagrams, to help children access and organize prior knowledge, as well as to help them connect this knowledge to new learning skills. In this way, teachers guide early readers to set a purpose for their reading so they can become more self-directed readers.

The challenge for teachers of early readers is finding the right balance between too easy and too difficult. If the text is too simple, the early reader will not feel challenged and will become bored. However, if the text is too difficult, the early reader will become frustrated and will lose interest. Children thrive when they are challenged to build upon skills they've already mastered. Early readers continue to develop the skills they honed on predictable texts at the emergent level. These children have graduated to the new challenges of the early reader.

Other young children, especially young second-language learners, seem to do best with texts that are less "bookish" and closer to spoken language. If language patterns are unfamiliar, even repetitive texts can present problems for some young readers. In a guided-reading program, teachers can vary text sequence and the level of prompts and supports needed to help all young readers become flexible and more confident as they handle many kinds of texts and language structures.

Yellow Umbrella Books: Early Level

Yellow Umbrella Books at this level are created especially for the early reader. The 36 student books for guided and independent reading have been leveled A (9-12) and B (13-16) to support strategic reading. The content-rich, high-interest material in these student books addresses national standards and benchmarks for social studies, math, and science. The 36 student books have been divided into three main groups, one for each subject: 12 social studies, 12 math, and 12 science. Six books in each subject are at level A, and six are at level B.

The 36 student books are accompanied by three content-related nonfiction big books. The nonfiction big books have been designed for

shared reading with a group; they may also be used by advanced readers for independent reading. These big books also correlate to national standards as they introduce and/or reinforce important social studies, math, and science concepts. By joining in on a shared-reading experience, early readers extend their familiarity with formal written language and text structures

This level of the Yellow Umbrella program also comes with a School-to-Home Book. This book contains black-and-white reproducibles of each student book. The reproducibles can be put together by children and brought home to extend the reading as children share the books with their families.

This comprehensive Teacher's Guide completes the Yellow Umbrella Early Level program. Each book is discussed at length, with strategies provided for introducing, reading, rereading, and discussing, as outlined below. The introductory box lists text features, supports, and challenges to help guide the reading lessons and activities. In addition, each book has a suggested reading-and-writing activity, as well as a school-to-home connection, and features a bibliography of related books, both nonfiction and fiction, depending on the topic.

The Teacher's Guide

This Teacher's Guide is intended to help teachers visualize what a guided-reading session might look like. The guide can also help teachers select appropriate books by familiarizing them with text features and teaching points that can be integrated into discussions. The best method of setting priorities, however, comes from observing children. Such observations will help teachers match books with children's current learning and reading levels.

Text Features, Challenges, and Supports

Level A and B texts provide strong supports for early readers. These supports include photographs that clearly illustrate concepts, consistent print placement, simple sentence structures, and high-frequency words, which serve as anchor words and promote self-monitoring of comprehension. These text supports ensure that children are not working out too many problems at once.

Each text also presents challenges. These challenges can be selectively addressed during the Preparing for Reading, Introducing the Book, or Teaching Points activities. For the early reader, challenges often focus on complex sounds, such as variant vowels and diphthongs. Other challenges include identifying noun and verb word endings, counting syllables, recognizing silent letters, and so on.

 ## Preparing for Reading

Before a book has been introduced to the group, it often helps to prepare children for the text they are about to read. Drawing on prior knowledge is a key preparatory activity, inviting children to share information and become familiar with the topic beforehand. In addition, implanting concept vocabulary will also make the reading more pleasurable. For example, if children are reading a book about money, writing the word *money* on the chalkboard and helping children to read and recognize it will implant the word and make it easier for children to recall the word when the book is presented.

 ## Introducing the Book

At this point in the lesson, the group sees the book for the first time. The group is offered the opportunity to read the title, discuss the cover photograph, and notice any additional text features, such as the author's name. Introducing the Book should include an open-ended discussion ("What do you think about . . ."), as well as questions that elicit predictions ("What do you think will happen . . ."). Children's answers can be recorded in graphic organizers to motivate reading.

 ## First Reading

A first reading often includes a picture-walk before actually tackling the text. Initially, the teacher leads the discussion, asking children to identify people, objects, and events in the photographs. The teacher might point to concept vocabulary words illustrated in the photographs and then challenge children to find those words in the text.

The reading begins with a quick review of the title page. Children are encouraged to recognize and read the book title, as well as to gather any new information from the photograph and, in the case of level B books, from the table of contents. The reading continues with the first page of text. Strategies for first readings will vary, depending on the topic, text structure, and photographs, as well as on children's prior knowledge. The First Reading section for each book suggests ideas, page by page, for effectively guiding children through the text.

If Preparing for Reading and Introducing the Book set the stage for reading, then the First Reading is the main event. Pointing out repetitive language patterns, modeling how to read difficult words, and prompting children to read on their own are all ways to direct, or guide, the group's reading.

 ## Rereading

As children work through the book, there may be particular phrasings or spellings that prove problematic. These words or text structures can be reviewed and reinforced in short lessons. Then children should read the book together. This can be done in a variety of ways. Children can read the book from cover to cover; they can take turns, reading in a "round-robin" fashion; they can read the book in pairs; or they can choose favorite pages to read aloud.

Whichever method is chosen, applaud children's attempts, and help them notice the effective strategies they already use. If necessary, participate in the reading, modeling fluent reading and problem-solving strategies. It also helps for children to make personal connections to the text and photographs.

Keep meaning at the forefront. Teach children

to confirm meaning by checking the photographs, and prompt them to go back and reread a sentence if it does not make sense. Praise fluent reading, and teach fluency by pointing out punctuation and natural phrasing in the text. Suggest that fluent reading sounds like "talking."

Discussing

After rereading the book, return to any lists or graphic organizers generated prior to reading. Together with the group, make additions or revisions to their initial thoughts. Also encourage children to express their impressions of the book, explaining why they enjoyed the content or language. Challenge children to retell the information or main idea of the book in their own words, as well as ask if they would like to learn more about the topic.

Taking running records and retelling with individual children are basic assessment strategies to all guided-reading programs. Small group discussions before, during, and after the reading provide ideal opportunities to assess children's prior knowledge and comprehension of the subject and text, as well as of children's current oral language and reading skills.

Teaching Points

In guided-reading groups, teachers can be flexible in meeting individual children's needs by prioritizing and focusing on a few teaching points at a time.

These points can be derived from the list of text features. How children perform during the first reading and interactions with children during rereading will inform teaching choices. Note where children had difficulty. Which strategies did or can they use to help themselves?

Children who are reading comfortably at text levels A and B are able to use analogy (onset and rime) to solve unknown words. They are ready to tackle more challenging spelling patterns, as well as to distinguish different sounds for similar patterns. For example, *look* and *cool* both have the letters *oo*, but the letters *oo* make completely different sounds in each word. The

early reader recognizes when he or she has mispronouced a word and is able to self-correct.

Word study expands children's vocabulary learning beyond memorizing a few items on a curriculum vocabulary list. Learning how to look at words and how to build on word meanings enables children to develop strategies for solving and learning words, which is the key to reading. With good examples of fluent reading and pronunciation, as well as with simple reading strategies, early readers are on their way to becoming not only proficient readers, but children who take an active delight in reading.

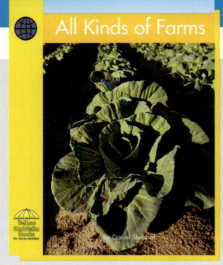

All Kinds of Farms

by Daniel Shepard

Standards and Benchmarks

See chart p. 86

Text Features

- **Word Count:** 146
- **High-Frequency Words:** *a, are, be, big, for, in, is, it, of, on, some, the, this, to, too*
- **Average Text Per Page:** 1-2 sentences, 4-15 words
- **Phonics/Word Study:** /ô/ with *r* (*corn, for, forest, oranges*); variant vowel /är/ –*arm* (*farm*), –*ar* (*are, harvest*); long /a/ –*ain* (*grain, rain*); short /e/ –*est* (*best, forest, harvest*); hard *g* and soft *g* (*grain, grow; orange*); hard *c* and soft *c* (*called, cool; places, rice*); variant vowel /ô/ –*all* (*called, small*); initial consonant blends *cr* (*cranberries*), *fr* (*fruit*), *gr* (*grains, grapes, ground, grow*); variant vowel /ur/, spelled *er* (*flower, under*); ending *y* (*many, paddy, ready*)

Supports

- Good photo/text support
- Draws on prior knowledge/previous experiences
- Consistent print placement
- Repetitive language pattern: *Some farms are ___.*

Challenges

- Verb ending –*ed* (*called, picked*)
- Plural endings: –*s* (*apples, bananas, farms, flowers, grains, grapes, kinds, oranges, pineapples, places, pumpkins*), –*es* (*potatoes, tomatoes*), –*ies* (*cranberries*)
- Various pronunciations of *ow*: (*flowers/grow*)
- Words with three syllables (*banana, cranberries, pineapples, potato, tomato*)
- Concept vocabulary: *bananas, cranberries, farm, juicy, paddy, pineapples, potato, rain forest, tomato, weather*

 ## Preparing for Reading

Display for the group a number of items that can be grown on a farm, such as flowers, an apple, a banana, and rice. Challenge children to explain what these items have in common, and lead them to the conclusion that each item was grown on a farm. Write the word *farm* on the board, and ask children to consider other plants that could be grown on a farm. Record children's ideas, perhaps within the circles of a word web. Allow children who live on farms or who have visited farms to share their experiences and first-hand knowledge.

 ## Introducing the Book

Present the book, and ask children how the item in the picture is similar to the items you shared with them. Confirm that the item is a plant that can be grown on a farm. Then ask children to find the word *Farm* in the book title, and have them read the entire title together. Speculate what this title suggests. Ask, "When you hear the words *all kinds of*, what do you think of?" Explain that as they read, they will learn about all kinds of—or different kinds of—farms. Predict with children how farms might differ, and jot down their ideas to check after reading.

 ## First Reading

Show children the title page, and ask them to read the title and identify the author's name. Ask children to explain what the items in the photograph have in common with the item on the book cover, and once again point out that these plants can be grown on a farm. Invite children familiar with farms to identify the plants. (They are corn plants.)

Let children respond to the pictures on pages 2 and 3. Allow time for children to predict the name of the food plants they see. Then have children read the text. Repeat the procedure with pages 4 and 5. Help children recognize the repeated pattern *Some farms are* on page 6.

Continue to read the book in this way, letting children identify and predict the words they might see on the page as well as recognizing the repeated language pattern. After reading the text on page 16, ask children where they have read the phrase *all kinds of farms*. (It is the book title.)

Rereading

Point out to children that they read about and saw not only all kinds of farms, but also the many different plants that can be grown on farms. Invite children to recall the plant words and write them on the board. Then say each word and ask a volunteer to find that word on the board and circle it. After this reinforcement practice, invite children to read the book back to you.

Discussing

Turn to page 16, and ask children to read the sentence. Then encourage them to describe the scene. Have them describe what the children might be seeing, hearing, touching, smelling, and perhaps even tasting. List children's words in a five-column sensory chart.

Then talk with children about how the things grown on farms can be described using the senses. For example, what does a pineapple look like? What does it feel like to touch? What does it taste like? Smell like? If possible, bring in samples of some of the plants from the book to enhance children's sensory explorations.

Teaching Points

Challenge children to build words from the word *farm*. Write *farm* on the board, and exaggerate the phonogram *–arm*. Have children change the first letter to create new words, such as *harm* and *charm*. Then ask children to change a last letter to make another new word and phonogram, such as *chart*. What new words can they create now? (*start, cart, part*) Change the last letter on *part* to make *park*. What new words can they make now? (*dark, shark, bark*)

Have children read the sentence on page 15.

Draw attention to two words with the same vowel spelling but different pronunciations— *grow* and *flowers*. Invite children to come up with other words with these sounds and spelling pattern. List the words in a two-column chart. For example: *crow, snow, blow, row, know; tower, power, towel, how, cow.*

Reading and Writing Connections

Have children create picture sentences, using the sentence starter *Some farms grow ___.* Pass out large index cards, and ask children to write the sentence starter, completing it with a drawing of a plant that grows on a farm. On the back of the index card, ask children to write the correct word. Have children share their cards, challenging classmates to identify the plant and then to read the word on the back of the card.

School-to-Home Connection

Invite children to bring home their School-to-Home book to share with their families. Encourage children to look through their homes for examples of foods that might have been grown on a farm, such as fruits or vegetables, and even flowers or houseplants. Ask children to draw their findings as a large collage, labeling each picture. At the top of the collage, have children write a few sentences about farms. Let children share and compare their collages in class.

Bibliography

Nonfiction

Ayers, Patricia. *Kid's Guide to How Fruits Grow.* New York: Rosen Publishing Group, 2003.

Gelman, Rita Golden. *Rice Is Life.* New York: Henry Holt and Company, Inc, 2000.

Fiction

Sloat, Teri. *Patti's Pumpkin Patch.* New York: Putnam Publishing Group, 1999.

At the Park

by Jeri Cipriano

Standards and Benchmarks

See chart p. 86

Text Features

- **Word Count:** 127
- **High-Frequency Words:** *a, are, at, can, for, from, go, have, in, see, some, the, to, we*
- **Average Text Per Page:** 1-2 sentences, 5-13 words
- **Phonics/Word Study:** variant vowel /är/ (*garden, park*); long /e/ –*eed* (*feed*), –*eep* (*sleep*); initial consonant blends *br* (*bring*), *fl* (*flowers*), *pl* (*places, play*), *sm* (*smell*), *sp* (*special*), *squ* (*squirrels*), *sw* (*swim, swing*); variant vowel /ô/ –*all* (*ball*), –*alk* (*walking*); /sh/, spelled *c* (*special*), digraph *th* (*paths, that, there*); long /a/ –*ake* (*lake*), –*ace* (*place*), –*ay* (*play*); long /i/ –*ide* (*ride*), –*igh* (*high*), –*ight* (*might*); long /u/ –*oo* (*zoo*), –*ood* (*food*); diphthong /ou/ –*ound* (*around, playground*)

Supports

- Good photo/text support
- Draws on prior knowledge/previous experiences
- Consistent print placement
- Repetitive language pattern: *Some parks have _____. We can _____.*

Challenges

- Text on pages 2, 15, and 16 does not follow repetitive language pattern
- Compound word: *playground*
- Text on page 7 has varied language pattern: *We might see _____.*
- Concept vocabulary: *flowers, gardens, lakes, park, paths, picnics, playgrounds, squirrels, tent*

 ## Preparing for Reading

Draw a word web on the board, and write the word *park* in the center circle. Read the word with the group. Invite children to identify places at a park or things they can do at a park, and list their ideas in the surrounding circles of the web. As children offer ideas, try to incorporate the language pattern of the book in your discussion. For example, if children suggest *ball fields*, you might say, "Some parks have ball fields. We can play ball at the park." Have children repeat these sentences with you so they become familiar with the text they will encounter in the book.

 ## Introducing the Book

Display the book for the group, and ask children to read the title to you. You might have them recognize the word *park* first and then encourage them to read the high-frequency words *at* and *the* on their own. Talk about the photograph, and invite children to describe the scenery. Encourage them to explain how the scenery reflects their ideas of a park. You might also speculate what the family in the photograph could be doing at the park.

 ## First Reading

Open the book to the title page. Have children recognize and read the title. Also point out the author's name and let children briefly talk about the photograph.

Turn to page 2, and ask children to find the word *park* in the sentence. Encourage them to point out any other words they recognize, and then read the entire sentence with them. Talk about the photograph, and then turn to page 3. Ask children to describe what the children in the picture are doing. Invite them to read the sentence to confirm their ideas.

Move on to page 4, and ask children to identify the park feature they see. Write this sentence starter on the board: *Some parks have ___.* Continue reading the sentence, and then turn to page 5 to discover what else people can do at parks with lakes. On page 6, point to the words you wrote on the board, making sure children recognize these words at the beginning of the sentence. As you continue through the book, let children predict what the sentence will be about as they study the picture. Make sure they recognize the repeated language pattern.

Rereading

Flip through the book, and encourage children to point out any words that were new or challenging, such as *special* on page 6. Write the word on the board, and invite children to read it with you as you run your finger under the letters. Ask children how the letter *c* in this word differs from other letter *c*s they've read. (It has the /sh/ sound.) After studying new words, invite children to read the book back to you.

Discussing

Return to the word web generated by the group before reading. Invite children to read their ideas, and discuss whether or not these park features or activities appeared in the book. Then talk about a local community park, and ask children to find pictures or ideas in the book that might show their own park experiences. Encourage children to express their ideas following the format of the book; for example, "Some parks have ___. Our park has ___." You could start a two-column comparison chart in which to record children's ideas.

Teaching Points

Say the word *park* with the group, and write it on the board. Ask children to find another word in the book with the *ar* spelling pattern, and say it with them—*garden*. Make sure children recognize the *r*-controlled sound. Then let children create new words from *park* by replacing the first letter: *bark, dark, Mark, shark*.

Invite children to go on a "scavenger hunt" through the book to find words with the initial consonant blends *sw, sp, sm, sl*, and *squ*. List chil-

dren's findings on the board, and read each word slowly, clearly enunciating each sound of the blend. Point out that readers pronounce each sound of these letter pairs—the letters do not form a new sound. You might start a chart of *s*-blends, inviting children to add words for each blend as they discover them on their own.

Reading and Writing Connections

Give each child in the group an index card, and ask them to complete this sentence: *We can ___ at the park.* Tell them to write their sentence on the card but not to show it to others. Then ask children to pantomime the action they wrote, encouraging the rest of the group to figure out the action. Have the group read the card to confirm their ideas.

School-to-Home Connection

Invite children to take home their School-to-Home book to read with their families. Encourage children to talk with their families about activities the family has enjoyed at a park, or that children have participated in with friends. Ask children to draw a picture of a park activity, and challenge children to write a sentence or two to tell about it. Suggest that children ask their families for assistance, if needed. Invite children to share their drawings with the group. You might combine their work into your own "At the Park" book.

Bibliography

Fiction

Browne, Anthony. *Voices in the Park.* New York: DK Publishing, 2001.

Mayer, Mercer. *Our Park.* Columbus, OH: McGraw-Hill Children's Publishing, 2001.

Sharratt, Nick. *Shark in the Park!* New York: Random House, 2002.

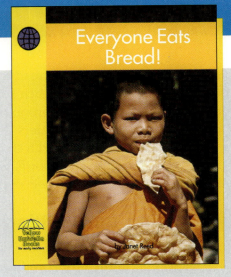

Everyone Eats Bread!

by Janet Reed

Standards and Benchmarks

See chart p. 86

Text Features

- **Word Count:** 139
- **High-Frequency Words:** *a, an, and, be, can, do, has, in, is, it, of, some, that, the, this, to, you*
- **Average Text Per Page:** 1-2 sentences, 4-16 words
- **Phonics/Word Study:** short /a/ *–an* (*can, pan*), *–at* (*flat*); long /a/ *–ade* (*made*), *–ake* (*baked, take*), *–ape* (*shaped, shapes*), *–ay* (*clay*); long /e/ *–eam* (*steamed*), *–eat* (*eat*); short /o/ *–ock* (*pocket*), *–ot* (*knot, pot*); initial consonant blends *r* (*bread, crunchy, fried*), *l* (*clay, flat*); silent consonants *k* (*knot*), *l* (*half*); ending blends *–ng* (*long*), *–nd* (*kind, round*), *–ft* (*soft*), *–ld* (*hold, world*); long /u/ *–ood* (*food*), *–oon* (*moon*)

Supports

- Good photo/text support
- Draws on prior knowledge/previous experiences
- Consistent print placement
- Repetitive language patterns: *Some people eat bread that is___. Some bread is ___.*
- Familiar adjectives (*long, thin, round, flat, crunchy, soft*)

Challenges

- Page 4 has three lines
- Various pronunciations: *oo* (*food, moon/look*), *ea* (*eat, steamed/bread*)
- Verb ending *–ed*: *baked, fried, rolled, steamed*
- Concept vocabulary: *bake, everyone, flat, fried, knot, oven, pocket, round, soft, steamed*

 Preparing for Reading

Pose the following riddle to the group: "I can be square or round, puffy or flat. You might see me at breakfast, lunch, or dinner. Who am I?" Guide responses by agreeing that it is a food. When someone correctly guesses *bread*, write the word on the board, and read it with the group. Invite children to exchange ideas about the different ways they've eaten bread, as well as the types of breads they've enjoyed. Record children's bread ideas to review after reading.

 Introducing the Book

Share the book with the group, and ask children to describe the bread they see on the cover. Challenge them to find the word *Bread* in the book title, and then ask them to read the entire book title. You might guide them through *Everyone* by covering up half of the word at a time so children can recognize the individual words. Also have children find and read the author's name.

 First Reading

Open the book to the title page, and let children respond to the photograph. Have them point to and describe the bread they see, and then ask them again to point to and read the book title and author's name.

On pages 2 and 3, have children find the bread, and then encourage them to read the sentences on their own. For pages 4 and 5, have children find the beginning and end of each sentence, making sure they identify the periods and beginning capital letters. Ask children what the pages have in common, and point out that they both discuss making bread in ovens. Moving on to pages 6 and 7, make sure children are able to recognize the repeated phrase *Some people eat bread that is.*

After reading pages 8 and 9, encourage children to read pages 10-15 on their own, recognizing the repeated phrase *Some bread is*, and then *This bread is.* Finishing with page 16, make sure children recognize this sentence as a question.

Rereading

Invite children to recall words in the book that describe bread, such as *half moon, knot, flat,* and *crunchy.* Refer to those pages, and have children find and read the words in the text; then point to the breads in the pictures and repeat the descriptive words. After reinforcing these words, ask children to return to the beginning of the book to read it again.

Discussing

Flip through the book with the group, and talk about the breads with which children are familiar. Encourage children to come up with specific names for the breads, if they know them; for example, the bread shaped like a knot on page 11 is a pretzel. The bread that is flat and soft and can be rolled up on page 14 is a tortilla. You might write the words on sticky notes to place on each photograph.

Discuss with children the organization of the book—it begins with how bread is made and then moves on to the shape of bread. Start a two-column chart, and ask children to recall information about how bread is made and the shape of bread for each column. Ask children how this organization helps them learn about bread.

Teaching Points

Turn to page 4 and ask children to find two words that have the spelling pattern *ea* (*eat* and *bread*). Say the words slowly, and ask children what they notice. Confirm that *ea* makes two different sounds. The *ea* in *eat* has the long /e/ sound, and the *ea* in *bread* has the short /e/ sound. Challenge children to come up with new words, substituting the initial consonants, for example: *head, dread, dead; seat, beat, treat, heat.*

Still on page 4, ask children to find two past-tense verbs—*baked* and *made.* Challenge them to come up with the present-tense verbs by saying the sentences: "Yesterday, I baked bread. Today I ___ bread. Yesterday, I made a sandwich. Today I ___ a sandwich." Write the present-tense verbs *bake* and *make* on the board. Help children notice that changing *make* to *made* is an irregular past tense because it does not follow the rule of adding *–ed*. Encourage children to dictate their own sentences to you using these verbs in both tenses.

Reading and Writing Connections

Have children fold a sheet of paper in half, and then in half again. When unfolded, the sheet should have four equal quadrants. Write the following sentence starters on the board: *Some people eat bread that is ___. I like bread that is ___.* Ask children to copy one or both sentence starters in each quadrant, and then challenge them to complete each. Tell children to illustrate their sentences, too. Demonstrate how to cut the quadrants apart on the fold lines, and then staple the quadrants together to make a mini-book.

School-to-Home Connection

Encourage children to take home their School-to-Home book to share with their families. Ask children to create a new mini-book describing the breads they find at home, such as slices of bread, bagels, muffins, pretzels, and so on. Then invite children to share their new mini-books with the group.

Bibliography

Nonfiction

Harbison, E.M. *Loaves of Fun: A History of Bread with Activities and Recipes from Around the World.* Chicago, IL: Chicago Review Press, 1997.

Morris, Ann. *Bread, Bread, Bread.* New York: William Morrow and Company, 1993.

Fiction

Dooley, Norah. *Everybody Bakes Bread.* Minneapolis, MN: Lerner Publishing Group, 1996.

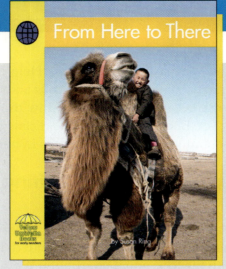

From Here to There

by Susan Ring

Standards and Benchmarks

See chart p. 86

Text Features

- **Word Count:** 179
- **High-Frequency Words:** *a, also, and, are, can, do, from, get, go, in, the, them, they, this, use, you*
- **Average Text Per Page:** 1 sentence, 10–14 words
- **Phonics/Word Study:** long /o/ –*oat* (*boat*), –*ow* (*row, snow*); long /i/ –*ide* (*ride*), –*ike* (*bike*), –*ile* (*while*), –*igh* (*high*), –*ight* (*might*), –*y* (*by, fly, sky*); variant vowel /är/ –*ar* (*car, far*), –*art* (*cart*), –*ark* (*market, park*); long /a/ –*ace* (*space*), –*ake* (*take*), –*ail* (*sail*), –*ain* (*train*); double consonants (*balloon, different, pull, shuttle*);

diphthong /ou/ –*ound* (*around, underground*), –*own* (*down, downtown*); long /e/ –*eas* (*easily*), –*eat* (*seat*), –*ee* (*see*), –*eep* (*deep*), –*eet* (*street*); initial consonant blends *r* (*from, street, through, trains, travel*), *s* (*sky, dogsled, snow, space*)

Supports

- Good photo/text support
- Familiar topic
- Consistent print placement
- Rhyming text

Challenges

- Text on pages 2 and 16 poses a question
- Text on page 16 has two sentences
- Compound words: *anywhere, dogsled, downtown, underground*
- Various pronunciations: *oa* (*boat/soar*), *ou* (*around, underground/through*), *ea* (*seat/Earth*)
- Variant vowel /âr/ has two spellings (*air, there*)
- Variant vowel /ô/ with *r* has two spellings (*horse, soar*)
- Inflected word endings –*le* (*buckled, cable, people, shuttle*), –*el* (*travel*)
- Concept vocabulary: *balloon, boats, buses, cable car, car, dogsled, horse, sail, space shuttle, taxi, trains, travel*

 Preparing for Reading

Ask children how they arrived at school that morning. Did they walk? Take a bus? Ride a bike? Get dropped off by car? Write children's answers on the board. Then ask, "How else could we get from here to there?" Brainstorm with children other modes of transportation, such as flying in airplanes, riding on trains, sailing on boats or ferries, and so on. If time allows, you might assign modes of transportation for children to draw and illustrate. This will help with one-to-one word correspondence and word meaning.

 Introducing the Book

Show children the book, and ask them to identify the object that helps the person pictured get "from here to there." When children suggest "camel," add the word to the list the group created. Then challenge them to read the book title on

their own, mentioning that you've said this phrase during the discussion. As children read the title, run your finger under each word. Also ask children to identify and read the author's name. Talk about the picture, asking children where in the world they think children would be able to ride a camel to get from here to there.

 First Reading

Open the book to the title page, and have children point to the title and author's name as they read them. Ask, "How are people getting from here to there in this picture?" Let children respond to the photo, encouraging them to explain if this is a mode of transportation they would like to try.

Move on to page 2, and ask children how the person in this photograph is getting from here to there. Then focus attention on the text, asking children to identify the type of sentence by its ending punctuation. To prevent the long question from intimidating children, suggest the strategy of covering the second line of text in order to concentrate on the first line.

Turn to page 3, and talk about the mode of transportation on this page. Ask children to find the term *hot air balloon* in the sentence, and then have them read the entire sentence. Continue through the book in this way, letting children study the photo and then finding the appropriate word in the text.

Rereading

Encourage children to share any modes of transportation that might have surprised them, such as the dogsled, the space shuttle, or the cable car. Help children read these new words, and then invite them to read the book again.

Discussing

Talk with children about how each method of traveling from here to there is appropriate for the landscape or terrain. For example, you might turn to page 5 and ask children if a dogsled would be a good mode of transportation for their area during the summer. When and where *is* it appropriate? Turning to page 6, you might ask children if they would take a plane to fly from their town to the next. When *would* it be appropriate? Let children have fun as they consider all aspects of traveling.

Teaching Points

Review the text on pages 8 and 9. Have children find a verb that changes from one page to the next (*ride* on page 8; *riding* on page 9). Challenge children to explain how the change was made, and make sure they recognize that the silent *e* at the end of *ride* was dropped and the verb ending *–ing* was then added.

Write the following words on the board: *people, shuttle, cable.* Ask children what these words have in common, and invite a volunteer to circle the *–le* at the end of each word. As a group, say

the /uhl/ sound made by *–le.* Then ask children to find two more words with this ending sound: *buckled, travel.* Point out that the *–el* in *travel* makes the same sound as *–le.*

Reading and Writing Connections

Ask children how the sentences in this non-fiction book differ from other nonfiction books they may have read, and confirm that the sentences rhyme. Invite children to copy the sentences from the book, leaving out the rhyming words. Have children write the rhyming words on individual index cards. Then display the rhyming sentence pairs, and challenge children to complete each sentence with the correct rhyming word card. Include all the word cards for the text. Invite children to read the sentences to you, listening to make sure the sentences sound right and make sense.

School-to-Home Connection

Invite children to take home their School-to-Home book to share with their families. At home, encourage children to play a transportation memory game. Instruct children to draw pictures of several individual vehicles on index cards, such as a boat, a plane, a train, a cable car, or a bike. On another card, have them write the word. Explain that they should then turn all the cards facedown. The object of the game is to match each picture with its correct word. Encourage children to share their cards with the group.

Bibliography

Nonfiction:

Kerrod, Robin. *Amazing Flying Machines.* New York: Dorling Kindersley/Alfred A. Knopf, 1992.

Lincoln, Margarette. *Amazing Boats.* New York: Dorling Kindersley/Alfred A. Knopf, 1992.

Lord, Trevor. *Amazing Bikes and Amazing Cars.* New York: Dorling Kindersley/Alfred A. Knopf, 1992.

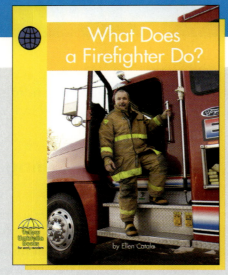

What Does a Firefighter Do?

by Ellen Catala

Standards and Benchmarks

See chart p. 86

Text Features

- **Word Count:** 136
- **High-Frequency Words:** *a, also, are, do, for, from, get, in, into, is, it, of, or, the, them, they, to, too, use, with, you*
- **Average Text Per Page:** 1-2 sentences, 5-13 words
- **Phonics/Word Study:** final *y* (*busy, carry, many, plenty, safety, very*); /k/, spelled *ck* (*check, sick, truck*); short /i/ –*ing* (*rings, things*); digraph *ch* (*check, children, teach*); digraph *th* (*other, thank, the, there, them, they, things, with*); three-letter consonant blend *spr* (*spray, spreading*); /z/, spelled *s* (*busy*); long /a/ –*ay* (*day, play, spray, ways*); long /u/ –*oo* (*too*), –*ool* (*tool*); variant vowel /är/ (*alarm, cars*); inflected ending –*en* (*children*); initial consonant blends *cr* (*crash*), *fr* (*from*), *tr* (*trees, truck*); variant vowel /ur/, spelled *er* (*firefighter, helicopter, other, water*); initial *a* (*about, alarm, around*)

Supports

- Good photo/text support
- High-interest topic
- Draws on some prior knowledge
- Consistent print placement
- Concept word *firefighters* appears at the beginning of sentences

Challenges

- Irregular plurals: *children, people*
- Distinction between plural ending –*s* (*cars, fires, firefighters, helicopters, things, tools, trees*) and verb ending –*s* (*rings*)
- Various pronunciations of *ea*: short /e/ (*spreading*), long /e/ (*teach*), variant vowel /ur/ (*learn*)
- Concept vocabulary: *alarm, fight, fire, spray, teach, truck, water*

 ## Preparing for Reading

Write the word *fire* on the board, and encourage children to identify words that describe a fire, such as *hot, flames, burning,* or *dangerous*. Then ask children who helps put out a fire, and write their answer on the board: *firefighter*. Invite a volunteer to come to the board to circle the word *fire* within the word. Help children read the word *fighter*, and point out that *firefighter* is a compound word—it is made up of two words. Ask children what questions they would ask a firefighter, if they could meet one. List children's questions on the board.

 ## Introducing the Book

Present the book to the group, and challenge children to find the word *Firefighter* in the title. After children have identified it, encourage them to read the entire title. Call attention to the ending punctuation mark, and ask children what purpose it serves. Confirm that a question mark appears at the end of a sentence that asks a question. Read the title question again, and review the list of questions children generated before reading. Point out questions they had about firefighters that also begin with the question word *what*.

 ## First Reading

Open the book to the title page, and have children identify not only the book title, but the author's name as well. Then talk about the picture. Speculate with children what new questions the picture raises, and write any new questions on the board.

Turn to page 2, and once again invite children to find the word *firefighter*. Ask children how the word here is slightly different, and confirm that it ends with *'s*. Briefly discuss that the *'s* shows possession; the text is describing the day of a firefighter, or a firefighter's day.

Move on to page 3. Again, encourage children to find the word *firefighters*, and then guide them through the text. Point out words with similar spelling patterns, such as *check* and *truck*. Continue through the book in this way, asking children to locate the word *firefighter* on each page, and then challenging them to read on their own, with prompts from you.

Rereading

Flip through the book, and encourage children to ask you to pause on pages they found the most interesting or enjoyable. Have children read those pages aloud. Make sure children are able to make connections between the text and the photographs. Then turn to the beginning of the book, and invite the group to read it again.

Discussing

Review with children the list of questions they had about firefighters. Invite children to read each question, and then discuss whether or not the question has been answered by reading the book. Encourage children to flip through the book to find the page on which the answer is found, sharing that page with the group. Then ask children if the book raised any new questions. For example, on page 8, children might wonder where the helicopter gets water to help put out a forest fire. Suggest that the group generate a new list of questions to perhaps ask a local firefighter in a letter or class visit.

Teaching Points

Invite children to scan the text to find words with the spelling pattern *–ay*. Write the words children find on the board (*day, spray, ways*), and have children say the words with you. Ask children what the words have in common, and conclude that the spelling pattern *ay* makes the long /a/ sound. Challenge children to replace the first letter of the words to come up with new words with the phonogram *–ay*, such as *bay, clay, hay, say, stay, pay, pray, okay, lay*, or *tray*.

Write the letters *–ing* on the board, and ask

children to find three words in the book that have this spelling pattern (*rings, things, spreading*). Challenge children to identify which *–ing* is a verb ending. Then start a two-column chart for children to record other words with the verb ending *–ing* as well as with the phonogram *–ing*, such as *running, walking, fighting; bring, sing, fling*.

Reading and Writing Connections

Ask children to copy the question *What does a firefighter do?* on a sheet of writing paper. Invite children to flip through the book for ideas and images they found exciting, and encourage them to answer the question by writing a sentence or two about the information in the book. Depending on the level of the group, children can copy or modify the text to reflect their ideas.

School-to-Home Connection

Encourage children to take home their School-to-Home book to share with their families. At home, have children look for ways that they help firefighters. For example, children could look for fire extinguishers and smoke alarms. For those children who live in apartments, suggest that they locate fire emergency exits. All children can work with families to map out a fire escape route in case of emergencies. Invite children to share their fire escape routes with the group.

Bibliography

Nonfiction

Demarest, Chris L. *Here Come Our Firefighters!* New York: Simon and Schuster Children's Publishing, 2002.

Gorman, Jacqueline Laks. *Firefighter.* Milwaukee, WI: Gareth Stevens Publishers, 2002.

Hayward, Linda. *Jobs People Do: A Day in the Life of a Firefighter.* New York: DK Publishing, 2001.

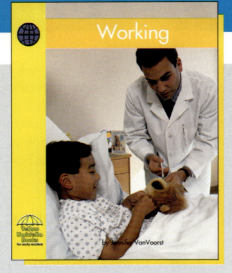

Working

by Jennifer VanVoorst

(*school*), *ck* (*sick, truck*); long /a/ –*afe* (*safe*), –*ace* (*place, space*), –*ake* (*makes*); long /u/ –*ood* (*food*), –*ool* (*school*); variant vowel /oo/ –*ood* (*wood*), –*ook* (*cook, look*); initial consonant blends *r* (*driver, grows, truck*), *l* (*explores, place*), *s* (*school, space, streets*); three-letter consonant blend *str* (*astronaut*); hard *c* and soft *c* (*care, carpenter, collector, cook; officer, place, police, space*)

Standards and Benchmarks

See chart p. 86

Text Features

- **Word Count:** 174
- **High-Frequency Words:** *a, are, as, at, do, for, from, go, he, in, man, of, she, the, this, to, us, we, you*
- **Average Text Per Page:** 1-2 sentences, 9-15 words
- **Phonics/Word Study:** variant vowel /är/ –*ar* (*carpenter, garbage*), –*arm* (*farmer*); variant vowel /ur/ spelled *er* (*carpenter, different, driver, farmer, keeper, officer, person, teacher*), *or* (*collector, work*), *ur* (*nurse*); /ô/ with *r* (*explores, morning*); /k/, spelled *ch*

Supports

- Good photo/text support
- Draws on prior knowledge/previous experiences
- Consistent print placement
- Repetitive language pattern: *This ___ works as a ___.*

Challenges

- Variation of language pattern on pages 2 and 3
- Question on page 16
- Various pronunciations: *or* (*morning/work*), *ea* (*teacher/learn*), *oo* (*cook/food*)
- Distinction between plural ending –*s* (*animals, kinds, sales, streets, things*) and verb ending –*s* (*builds, explores, grows, helps, keeps, makes, moves, takes, works*)
- Concept vocabulary: *astronaut, carpenter, cook, dentist, garbage collector, nurse, police officer, teacher, works*

 ## Preparing for Reading

Invite children to help you finish these sentences: *At school, we do school [work]. At home, we do home [work]. In art class, we do art [work].* Ask children what all these terms have in common, and write the word *work* on the board. Encourage children to explain what the word *work* means to them. Who else works? List the workers children suggest, as well as the work or jobs they do, in a two-column chart with the headings *Workers* and *The Work They Do.*

 ## Introducing the Book

Display the book for the group, and invite a volunteer to point to the root word *work* on the cover. Encourage children to read the entire word, *working*. Ask, "Who is working in the picture? What type of work is he doing?" Review the two-column chart to see if the children suggested a similar worker and job. Then speculate what children might expect to learn in a book entitled *Working*.

 ## First Reading

Open the book to the title page, and have children read the book title together. Challenge them to identify the worker and to describe the work he is doing. Then move on to pages 2 and 3. Let children describe the workers in the pictures, and then read the sentences with them. Remind children that they've listed "many different kinds of work" in their two-column chart. Which kinds of work do they predict they might read about?

Read pages 4 and 5 with the group. Discuss the language pattern, helping children notice that the first sentence identifies the worker; the second sentence explains the worker's job. Ask, "What does this man work as? What does this woman work as?" Invite children to answer using the language pattern from the book.

Continue with pages 6 and 7. Before reading, ask children to predict the word for each worker, based on the photograph. As children read the text, be sure they recognize the repeated language pattern and organization. Repeat this reading process as you navigate the book.

Rereading

Challenge children to recall the names of the workers they read about, and write the names on the board, such as *police officer, garbage collector, teacher, astronaut*. As you write each word, say it aloud, clearly enunciating letter groups. Then point to each word and ask children to flip through the book to find the page on which that word appears. Now that children have become more familiar with the words, invite them to read the book again, this time on their own.

Discussing

Share with children that a conclusion is a sentence or two that explains what they have learned after reading. Encourage children to come up with conclusions they can make about working. Lead children to such ideas as, "There are many different types of jobs. Many jobs help others. People are needed to do most jobs."

Then take a class poll to find out which jobs children think would be exciting. Let children vote on three different jobs featured in the book. Discuss the results of the vote and encourage children to draw further conclusions about the group's job preferences.

Teaching Points

Have children look through the book for words that end with –s. Help children sort the words according to the function of the word ending: plural-ending –s or verb-ending –s. Help children realize the different uses of each by dictating sentences with each word. Ask children to circle words and underline the ending –s.

Write the following words with the suffix –er on the board: *teacher, farmer, driver*. Cover up the suffix, and have children read the word that remains. Work with children to come up with

sentences that tell about the jobs and workers; for example: *A farmer farms. A teacher teaches. A driver drives.* Then ask children to think of other professions that begin with a verb and add the suffix –er, such as *manager, waiter, singer, builder, player*, or *writer*.

Reading and Writing Connections

Encourage children to think of a job not mentioned in the book that someone could do. Pass out drawing paper, and ask each child to draw a picture of the worker. Below the picture, ask them to write two sentences, modeled after those in the book: *This ___ works as a ___. (He/She) ____.* After children share their work, collect the pages and compile them in a group book.

School-to-Home Connection

Encourage children to bring home their School-to-Home book to share with their families. Invite them to interview someone they know about the work he or she does. Ask children to draw a picture of the person and then write a caption based on the book text: *This is ___. (He/She) works as a ___. (He/She) ___.* Tell children to ask family members for help with writing new words. In class the next day, encourage children to share their pictures and sentences with the group.

Bibliography

Nonfiction

Hayward, Linda. *Jobs People Do* series, including *A Day in the Life of a Builder... a Teacher... a Dancer... a Doctor*. New York: DK Publishing, 2001.

Pedersen, Marika. *Mommy Works, Daddy Works*. Toronto, Ontario: Annick Press, 2000.

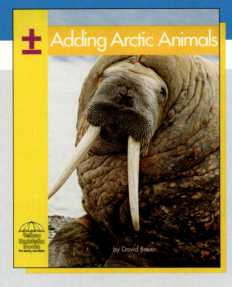

Adding Arctic Animals
by David Bauer

/ô/ with r, –or (for), –ore (shore), –ar (warm); variant vowel /oo/, –oo (food, too), –ou (caribou); variant vowel /âr/, –are (hare), –ear (bear); silent e (alone, come, female, hares, have, here, live, male, one, place, shore, some, white, wolves)

Supports

- Good photo/text support
- Interactive text
- Consistent print placement
- One line of text on some pages
- Repetitive language pattern: Add the ___.

Challenges

- Math equations as part of text
- Proper noun: Arctic
- Words with three syllables: animals, caribou
- Various pronunciations: ar (Arctic/warm/caribou/polar), oo (food/looks)
- Homonyms: to, too, two
- Irregular plural: wolves
- Distinction between verb ending –s (looks) and plural ending –s (animals, bears, hares, herds, others, seals)
- Concept vocabulary: Arctic, babies, caribou, female, foxes, hare, harp seal, musk oxen, ocean, polar bear, wolves

Standards and Benchmarks

See chart pp. 88

Text Features

- **Word Count:** 120
- **High-Frequency Words:** a, can, come, for, have, in, is, of, on, some, the, their, they, to, too, up, we, with
- **Average Text Per Page:** 1-2 sentences, 5-11 words
- **Phonics/Word Study:** initial /w/ (warm, water, we, winter, wolves); x (oxen, foxes); variant vowel /ur/, spelled er (herds, others, summer, together, winter), ar (polar), ur (fur); hard c and soft c (Arctic, can, caribou, cold, come; place); variant vowel /är/ (Arctic, harp);

 ## Preparing for Reading

Write the following animal names on the board, and say the names as you write them: *polar bear, arctic hare, wolf, fox, caribou, musk ox, harp seal, walrus.* Point to each word, and ask children to read the name with you. Then ask children if they know where all these animals live, and confirm that it is the Arctic. Display a world map, and show children where the Arctic is. Ask children what they think the weather is like there, and point out that it is cold and snowy. Then invite children to share anything they know about these animals.

 ## Introducing the Book

Distribute the books to the group, and ask children which arctic animal they see on the cover. Ask children how they know it is a walrus, and confirm that walruses have long tusks. Then invite children to find the word *Arctic* in the book title. Because all the words begin with a capital *a*, this

task might prove challenging. Suggest, therefore, that children look for a word with the ending sound /k/. Does the first word have a letter that makes the /k/ sound? What about the last word? How about the middle word? Yes! The letter *c* can make the /k/ sound. Read the entire title with them; then talk about what the word *Adding* tells them about the book.

 ## First Reading

Pause at the title page, and help children read the title again. Have them identify the animal as a polar bear, and comment if the bear matches the descriptions children offered before reading.

Have children find the word *Arctic* on page 2, and then speculate which other words they might find in the text, such as *cold* and *animals.* After children scan the text for familiar words, encourage them to read the sentences. Continue with page 3, and then talk about the format of pages 4 and 5. Let children identify the animals on each page, and then invite them to read the text. Ask children to point to features that are different from most sentences, and call attention to the equation. Tell children to "read" the equation, saying the words for each number and symbol: one plus two equals three.

Turn to pages 6 and 7, and ask children if these two pages are similar in format to pages 4 and 5. Have children identify the parts that are similar. Also ask them to explain how the pages are different (different animals, different numbers). Before moving on, tell children that they can follow this format as they read the rest of the book.

Rereading

Invite children to stump you with animal names from the book. Tell children to turn to any page, challenging you to name the animal. Say a name that is not correct, and have children correct you by finding the correct word in the text. Then invite children to read the book again on their own.

Discussing

Write the first half of each math equation on the board, and challenge children to look through the book for its answer. Complete the equation with their answer, and then ask children if the equation and the answer match. To check their answers, tell children to count the animals on both pages. Ask children if they think this is a fun way to practice adding.

Teaching Points

Remind children that they were able to recognize the word *Arctic* in the book title by concentrating on the /k/ sound, spelled *c*. Ask children to look through the book for other words with the /k/ sound, spelled *c*, and have volunteers write the words on the board. Say the words with the group to confirm their ideas. Encourage children to suggest other words, finding ideas around the classroom. If the word is not spelled with *c*, help children learn the correct spelling.

Have children study the book title, and challenge them to identify the word that is a verb. Write the word *adding* on the board, and call attention to the verb ending *–ing*. Have children say a sentence with this word, such as, "We are adding arctic animals." Then invite children to make new sentences with other *–ing* verbs. For example, "We are reading a book. We are learning to read. We are having fun."

Reading and Writing Connections

Working with partners, encourage children to write new pages for the book. Assign an arctic animal to each pair. Encourage children to come up with things that their animals could do, such as swim, slide on the ice, sleep, dig in the snow, and so on. Have children write sentences, including the math equations, modeled after those in the book, but without the answers. Invite partners to share their work with the group, asking the group to figure out the answers.

School-to-Home Connection

Invite children to take home their School-to-Home book to read with their families. Suggest that children create a mobile of arctic animals. Explain that they can include more than one animal for each mobile cutout. Once the mobile is complete, ask children to write a sentence and a math equation on a separate sheet of paper, following the language pattern of the book. Encourage them to share their mobiles with the group.

Bibliography

Fiction

Capucilli, Alyssa Satin. *Mrs. McTats and Her Houseful of Cats.* New York: Margaret K. McElderry Books, 2001.

Murphy, Stuart J. *Animals on Board.* New York: HarperCollins, 1998.

Root, Phyllis. *One Duck Stuck.* Cambridge, MA: Candlewick Press, 2003.

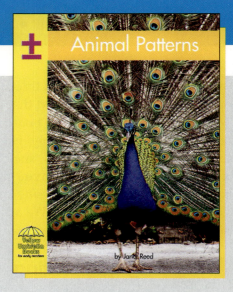

Animal Patterns

by Janet Reed

vowel /ô/ –*all* (*all, called*); variant vowel /ur/, spelled *ar* (*leopard*), *er* (*butterfly, pattern, spiders, tiger, under*), *ur* (*fur*); initial *s* blends *sp* (*spiders, spots*), *str* (*stripes*); double consonants (*all, butterfly, called, guess, patterns*); digraph *th* (*the, there, these, they, this*)

Supports

- Good photo/text support
- High-interest topic
- Interactive text
- Consistent print placement
- One or two lines on most pages
- Repetitive language patterns: *This ___ has a pattern. Which of these ___ has a pattern?*

Challenges

- A mix of sentences and questions
- Two sentences on pages 3, 5, 13, and 16
- Three lines on page 3
- Words with three syllables: *animals, butterfly*
- Compound words: *butterfly, honeycomb, ringtail*
- Irregular plural noun: *deer*
- Plural ending –*s*: *animals, dogs, bees, horses, kinds, patterns, snakes, spiders, spots, stripes, trees, wings, zebras*
- Concept vocabulary: *fur, honeycomb, pattern, spots, stripes, web*

Standards and Benchmarks

See chart p. 88

Text Features

- **Word Count:** 130
- **High-Frequency Words:** *a, all, are, can, do, does, has, have, in, is, its, of, on, or, the, they, this, too, you*
- **Average Text Per Page:** 1-2 sentences, 5-17 words
- **Phonics/Word Study:** long /a/ –*ake* (*make, snakes*); short /u/ (*bug, butterfly, until*); short /i/ –*ing* (*ringtail, wings*); long /i/ (*kinds, spider, tiger*), CVCe (*stripes*); long /e/ –*ee* (*honeybees, trees*); /w/, spelled *w* (*web, wings*), *wh* (*what, when, which, why*); variant

 ## Preparing for Reading

The night before you plan to share the book with the group, choose to wear a shirt, sweater, jacket, or pants that has a recognizable pattern, such as stripes, plaids, or spots. In class, draw attention to your clothing, and encourage children to describe the pattern. Have them identify colors, listing the colors in pattern order. Challenge children to identify the pattern, and write the correct term on the board. Then speculate with children where else they might see patterns. Let children view their own clothing, as well as any patterned displays around the room.

 ## Introducing the Book

Share the book with the group, and encourage children to respond to the cover photograph. Invite children who know this bird to identify it as a peacock. Then challenge children to describe the patterns on the peacock's tail feathers. Elicit color as well as shape words. Then help children read the book title. You might cover up most of the title, revealing small chunks at a time to focus attention: *An-i-mal Pat-ter-ns.* Let children suggest other animals that have patterns, and list their ideas on the board to review after reading.

 ## First Reading

Let children comment on the title-page photograph. Review the list of animals children named prior to reading, and note if *snake* was one of them. Then point to the title, and have children read it on their own.

Move on to page 2. Ask children to identify the animal. Have them sound out the word *tiger*, naming the letters. Then ask children to look at the text. Do they see a word on the page that could be *tiger*? Confirm children's ideas, and then invite them to read the entire sentence to you. You might need to guide them through the three-letter blend *str* in *stripes*.

Lead children to read and explore the book in this way, identifying the animal, thinking about the letters that make up the word, and then identifying the word in the text. For this reading, concentrate mainly on the words, not on children's responses to the patterns or pictures. Encourage children to focus on reading the questions on pages 8 through 12; they can answer the questions after reading, during the discussion.

Rereading

Write animal names on the board, and have children read them. To build comprehension and word recognition, ask children to find the page in the book that has that animal. Then ask children to read the book again.

Discussing

Now that children have become comfortable with the text, choose pages in the book to discuss more fully. For example, turn to page 5, and invite children to recall the name of this animal. Write the word *ringtail* on the board, and make sure children recognize the two words that make up this compound word. Then ask children why this animal is called a ringtail, and have them describe the pattern on its tail. Have children turn to page 8 and read the question. Encourage them to describe the zebras' pattern. Let children read and answer the questions on the pages that follow, and then let them have fun answering the question on page 16.

Teaching Points

Write the following words from the book on the board: *what, when, which, why*. Ask children to say the words with you. Encourage them to exaggerate the beginning sound, and invite a volunteer to circle the letters that make the sound. Make sure they include the letter *h*. Then ask children what else these words have in common, and confirm that they are question words. Have children practice asking questions with these words.

Reading and Writing Connections

Invite children to think of some items that could have a pattern or not, such as a shirt, a blanket, or a book jacket. Pass out drawing paper, and ask children to choose an item and draw it twice: once with a pattern and once without. Then have children write questions, modeled after those in the book: *Which of these _____ has a pattern?* Have children pass their drawings around the group for group members to read and answer.

School-to-Home Connection

Invite children to take home their School-to-Home book to read with their families. Then ask children to look around their homes for patterns. Ask children to a draw the object with the pattern, and challenge them to write a sentence about it. For example: *This couch has a pattern of stripes.* Encourage children to create a separate page for each patterned object they find. Then tell children to combine their pages into their own book of patterns, and have children read their books to the group.

Bibliography

Nonfiction

Stockdale, Susan. *Nature's Paintbrush: The Patterns and Colors Around You.* New York: Simon and Schuster Children's Publishing, 1999.

Swinburne, Stephen R. *Lots and Lots of Zebra Stripes: Patterns in Nature.* Honesdale, PA: Boyds Mills Press, 2002.

Fiction

Shields, Carol Diggery. *Patterns.* Brooklyn, NY: Handprint Books, 2001.

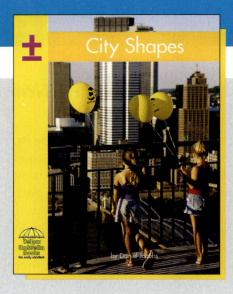

City Shapes

by Daniel Jacobs

tall), –alk (*sidewalk*); /ô/ with r (*court, doors*); variant vowel /oo/ (*look*); digraph sh, initial (*shapes, shop*), final (*whoosh*); digraph ch, final (*much*); hard c and soft c (*can, circles, colorful, count, rectangle; circles, city*); ending y (*busy, city*)

Supports

- Good photo/text support
- Interactive text
- Consistent print placement
- Two lines of text on most pages
- One sentence on page 5

Challenges

- No repetitive language pattern
- A mix of sentences and questions on almost every page
- Three lines of text on pages 8, 12, and 15
- Words with three syllables: *basketball, colorful, different, rectangles, triangles*
- Compound words: *basketball, inside, sidewalk, sometimes*
- Various pronunciations: oo (*look/too/door*), ou (*you/count/court*)
- Irregular spelling for short /i/: ui (*buildings*), u (*busy*)
- Concept vocabulary: *bridge, building, circles, city, colorful, doors, rectangles, shape, sidewalk, sign, squares, triangle*

Standards and Benchmarks

See chart p. 88-89

Text Features

- **Word Count:** 176
- **High-Frequency Words:** *a, and, are, at, can, do, for, has, have, in, is, of, on, see, so, the, them, this, to, too, you*
- **Average Text Per Page:** 2 sentences, 9-15 words
- **Phonics/Word Study:** inflected word endings –le (*circle, rectangle, triangle*), –es (*houses*); diphthong /ou/ (*count, houses*); long /i/ –ind (*behind, find, kind*); /kw/ (*squares*); variant vowel /ô/ –all (*basketball,*

 ## Preparing for Reading

Invite four volunteers to come to the board. Ask each to draw a shape—a square, a circle, a triangle, and a rectangle—and have children explain what is special about each shape. (For example, a circle has all curved sides; a triangle has three sides and three corners; rectangles and squares have four sides and four corners.) Then challenge children to look around the room for objects with these shapes. Help them draw the conclusion that these shapes can be found on many objects in many places.

 ## Introducing the Book

Share the book with the group, and invite children to respond to the cover photograph. Ask children what kind of community it shows. Is it a small town? A farm community? A large city? Have children point to objects in the photo that identify the place as a large city. Encourage them to identify the shapes they see, too. Then

read with the group the book title, helping them through letters that might be new to them, such as the soft c in *city* and the digraph sh in *shapes*.

 ## First Reading

After children have read the book title on the title page and explored the picture, move on to pages 2 and 3. Have them find the word *city* on each page, and encourage them to read the text.

Turn to pages 4 and 5, and ask children which shape they think these pages will be about. Write the shape word children suggest. Then invite them to read, look, and listen for their shape ideas. Guide children through the book in this way, exploring the shapes on each spread: circles on pages 6 and 7, rectangles on pages 8 and 9, and triangles on pages 10 and 11.

Prepare children for the rest of the book by explaining that they are going to see a combination of shapes in these city scenes. Remind children that if they are not sure of a shape word, they can look to the photograph for clues. Invite children to continue reading.

Rereading

Have children flip through the book and choose city scenes they liked. Encourage children to describe these scenes in their own words, using the correct shape terms. Then ask children to read the book again to you.

Discussing

Ask children if they think a city is a good place to see shapes, and invite children to share their ideas. Then talk about the function of these shapes. For example, why is a circle a good shape for a basketball hoop? (Because a basketball is a circular shape, or a sphere.) Why are triangles good shapes for roofs? (Because rain and snow can slide right off.) Why are rectangles good shapes for tall buildings? (Because square rooms fit well into rectangular buildings.)

Then consider with children the shapes of buildings and other features around their local area. For example, what shape is the school? How would the school be different if it was shaped like a triangle? Like a circle? Let children have fun with their ideas as they explore shapes around them.

Teaching Points

Help children explore how the letter *r* can change a word when placed after a vowel. Write the word *at* on the board, and have the group read it aloud. Then invite a volunteer to insert the letter *r* between the *a* and the *t*, and read the new word: *art*. Say the word several times to help children hear the influence of the letter *r* on the vowel.

Then point out to children words in the book with vowels that are followed by the letter *r*. First, write the word *count* on the board and say it for the group. As children watch, erase the *n* and replace it with an *r*. Read the new word,

exaggerating the *r* sound: *court*. Look around the room for other words with an *r*-controlled sound. Write the words on the board and say them with the group, exaggerating the /r/ sound as before.

Reading and Writing Connections

Remind children of the classroom objects they explored before reading that had identifiable shapes. Working with a partner, ask children to go on their own shape search, looking for shapes in new ways now that they have read the book. Tell children to draw the object and identify the shape by writing this sentence: *I see a ___ in the ___.* Have children share their shapes and read their sentences to the group.

School-to-Home Connection

Invite children to take home their School-to-Home book to read with their families. Instruct children to create their own cityscape. Tell children to draw a shape featured in the book and have a family member use that shape as a starting point for drawing a building, lake, car, boat, or other item. Encourage them to take turns drawing the shapes and developing them into something larger. Invite children to share their drawings with the group.

Bibliography

Nonfiction

Hoban, Tana. *Shapes, Shapes, Shapes.* New York: William Morrow and Company, 1995.

MacDonald, Suse. *Sea Shapes.* San Diego, CA: Harcourt, 1998.

Fiction

Bryant, Megan E. *Shape Spotters.* New York: Penguin Putnam Books for Young Readers, 2002.

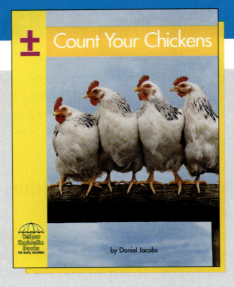

Count Your Chickens

by Daniel Jacobs

(*know*); digraph *th* (*that, the, them, these, there, they, things, this*); digraph *ch* (*chickens, chicks, much*); long /ī/, spelled *y* (*by, fly*); short /u/ –*un* (*fun, sun*), –*one* (*one, done*); variant vowel /âr/ –*air* (*pair*), –*ere* (*there*); variant vowel /är/ (*are, arms, star*); silent *e* (*are, five, geese, here, there, these, whole*)

Standards and Benchmarks

See chart p. 89

Text Features

- **Word Count:** 123
- **High-Frequency Words:** *a, all, also, and, are, as, at, by, can, do, has, if, in, is, it, so, that, the, them, they, this, to, too, up, you, your*
- **Average Text Per Page:** 1-2 sentences, 4-10 words
- **Phonics/Word Study:** /k/, spelled *k* (*look, make*), *ck* (*chickens, chicks*), *c* (*can, coop, count*); variant vowel /oo/, spelled *oo* (*coop*), *ou* (*group, you*); silent *k*

Supports

- Good photo/text support
- Interactive text
- Familiar images
- Consistent print placement
- Rhyming text

Challenges

- A mix of words and numbers
- Three sentences and three lines of text on page 16
- Homonyms: *two, too, to*
- Various pronunciations: *ou* (*group/count*), final *y* (*many/by, fly*), *ow* (*how/know*)
- Irregular plural: *geese*
- Plural ending –*s*: *arms, chickens, chicks, fingers, things, toes, twins, ways*
- Concept vocabulary: *again, chicks, chickens, count, fingers, geese, group, sea star, toes*

 ## Preparing for Reading

Write the term *skip count* on the board, and ask children if they know what it means. After eliciting ideas, confirm that when people skip count, they skip certain numbers when counting. To show children what you mean, hold up all the fingers of one hand, and ask children how many fingers you are holding up. When children quickly identify five, hold up your other hand, and ask children how many fingers you are holding up now. After children identify both five and ten, ask them which numbers they skipped. Point out that they have skip counted by 5s.

 ## Introducing the Book

Present the book to the group, and have children count and identify the animal. Ask, "Can you skip count these chickens by two?" Point to the first two chickens, encouraging children to say, "two." Point to the next two chick-ens, and have children say, "four." Ask, "If two more chickens were in the picture, what would the next number be?" Then have children find the word *Chickens* in the book title, and help them read the entire title.

 ## First Reading

Have children read the book title on the title page, and then ask them how they could skip count the feet and toes in the picture. Children might offer counting the feet by 2s, counting the children by 2s, or counting the toes by 5s or 10s. Explain to children that as they read this book, they will discover different ways to skip count.

Encourage children to read the text on pages 2 and 3. Tell them to say the numbers just as they would words. Ask children what they notice about the text, and confirm that it rhymes. Write the rhyming words *one* and *done* on the board.

Then have children move on to pages 4 and 5. As they read the text aloud, make sure they also read aloud the numbers. Have children continue with pages 6 and 7, and then pages 8 and 9. On pages 10 and 11, children will once again see numbers mixed with the words. Continuing with pages 12 and 13, children might hesitate over the word *forty*. Ask them to notice and read the familiar spelling pattern *for*, and then to add the common letter sounds for *t* and final *y*. Help children manage the text on page 16 by suggesting that they locate the beginning and ending of each sentence.

Rereading

Because children were concentrating on reading, they might not have heard or enjoyed the rhyming text. Tell children to follow along in their books as you read the text to them, encouraging them to pay attention to the rhyming words and rhythm of the language. This is a good time for them to learn through modeling from you. Afterward, ask children to read the book again.

Discussing

Encourage children to explain the main idea of this book, and confirm that the book shows them a few different ways to skip count. Have children explain the skip-counting numbers, referring to each photograph, as you write the numbers on the board: by 2s: 2, 4, 6, 8, 10; by 5s: 5, 10, 15, 20, 25, 30, 35, 40; and by 10s: 10, 20, 30, 40, 50, 60.

Then challenge children to continue each skip-counting pattern, perhaps going around the group in order and asking children to supply the next number. Help children brainstorm ideas of things in the classroom they could skip count.

Teaching Points

Use the word *chicken* to review the /ch/ sound. Write the word *chicken* on the board, and underline both *ch* and *ck*. Point out that these spelling patterns are similar. Make the /ch/ sound, say *chicken*, and invite a volunteer to circle the letters that make /ch/. Then point to two items in the room, one with /ch/ and the other without, and

ask children to identify the correct /ch/ word. For example: *chalk* and *pencil*; *check mark* and *star*; *chair* and *desk*; *chalkboard* and *bulletin board*; *cherry* and *apple*. Write the /ch/ words on the board to confirm children's word choices.

Reading and Writing Connections

Consider with children the classroom items they suggested that could be skip-counted. Assign one item to partners, and ask children to write a few sentences that tell about it. Tell them to include numbers in their sentences, too. For example: "We can count by 2s the number of kids in class: 2, 4, 6, 8, 10." Invite partners to read their sentences to the group.

School-to-Home Connection

Invite children to take home their School-to-Home book to read with their families. With their families, ask children to look through magazines for pictures with multiple items that they could skip count, such as groups of flowers or animals or books. Have children cut out the picture and attach it to a sheet of paper with glue or tape. Have them write a sentence about how to skip count the items (by 2s, 5s, or 10s). Encourage children to share their ideas with the group.

Bibliography

Nonfiction

Good Apple. *Wipe-Away Books: Skip Counting by 5's and 10's.* Columbus, OH: McGraw-Hill Children's Publishing, 2000.

Fiction

Arenson, Roberta. *One, Two, Skip a Few.* New York: Barefoot Books, 1998.

MacKain, Bonnie. *One Hundred Hungry Ants.* Boston, MA: Houghton Mifflin Company, 1999.

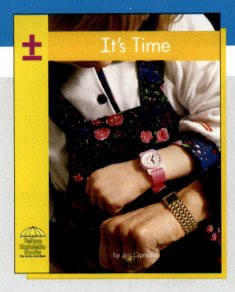

It's Time

by Jeri Cipriano

Standards and Benchmarks

See chart p. 89

Text Features

- **Word Count:** 175
- **High-Frequency Words:** *a, also, an, and, are, can, do, has, in, is, it, of, to, we, you, your*
- **Average Text Per Page:** 1-2 sentences, 7-15 words
- **Phonics/Word Study:** short /a/ –*and* (*and, hand*); long /a/ –*ake* (*bake, take, takes*), –*ame* (*game*), –*ay* (*day, days, holidays, play*); long /i/ –*ime* (*time*), –*ie* (*tie*); long /o/ –*ow* (*grow, know, show*); /k/, spelled *k* (*kiss, take, takes, weeks*), *c* (*can, cookies, second*), *ck* (*clocks, kick*); /sh/, spelled *sh* (*shoes, short, show*), *s* (*measure*); diph-

thong /ou/ (*about, hours*); variant vowel /ô/ –*all* (*ball, tall*), –*ong* (*long*); initial *y* (*years, you, your*); final consonant blends –*nd* (*and, end, hand, seconds*), –*ng* (*beginning, everything, long, thing*)

Supports

- Some photo/text support
- Draws on prior knowledge
- Consistent print placement
- One or two lines on most pages
- Repetitive language patterns: *It takes about a ___ to ___. We can measure time in ___.*

Challenges

- Three sentences on page 5
- Three lines of text on pages 4, 5, 7, 8, 12, 15, and 16
- Words with three syllables: *beginning, celebrate, different, everything, favorite*
- Long /i/ spelling pattern, short /i/ sound: *favorite*
- Long /u/ spelling pattern, short /i/ sound: *minute*
- Various pronunciations of *ou: about/you/your*
- Distinction between verb ending –*s* (*takes*) and plural ending –*s* (*cookies, days, hours, minutes, months, seconds, shoes, things, weeks, years*)
- Concept vocabulary: *days, hours, measure, minutes, months, seconds, time, weeks, years*

 ## Preparing for Reading

Tell children that you are going to ask them to do some simple things, and you will measure the amount of time it takes them to do it. Explain that this activity is not a race. Then pass out drawing paper and ask children to draw a square. How long did it take them? On the back side, ask them to draw a house. Which drawing took longer to make? Then ask children to fold the paper in half. How much time did it take? Tell children to continue folding to make a paper airplane. How much time did they need now? Show children the tool you used to measure the time, such as a stopwatch or the second hand on the classroom clock. Share the times with the group for children to compare.

 ## Introducing the Book

Before handing out the books, cover up the book title with sticky notes. Challenge children to figure out what the book is about by studying the photograph. Ask, "Which two objects are the main focus of the picture? What do watches help us to do?" Tell children to remove the sticky notes, and invite them to read the book title to confirm their ideas. Then have children describe how you used time to measure the activities they just completed.

 ## First Reading

Invite children to open the book to the title page. Have them read the title and point to the clock in the photograph.

Encourage children to begin reading. If children stumble over *everything* on page 2, point out that this word is a compound word. Children might also struggle with *measure* on page 5. Explain that the letters *ea* make the short /e/

sound, and the letter *s* makes the /sh/ sound. Help children read the word *second* on pages 5 and 6, explaining that the letter *c* makes the /k/ sound. You might also mention that *minute* on page 7 has two short /i/ sounds. Write these unusual words on the board for children to become familiar with them.

Rereading

Have children recall words that measure time, and write them on the board as children say them. Encourage children to practice reading and saying these words to you. Then invite children to turn to the beginning of the book to read again.

Discussing

Work with the group to create a chart that shows which activities take similar amounts of time. For example, in a column labeled *Seconds*, children should suggest "kick a ball," "raise your hand," and "give a kiss." In a column labeled *Minutes*, children should note "tie your shoe." Then ask children to think of other activities that take them about a second to do, such as waving hello, jumping once, clapping their hands. What might take them a minute to do? What might take them an hour to do? What takes so long that the time is hard to measure?

Review with children the tools they can use to measure time, such as clocks, watches, stopwatches, and timers. Speculate with children why it is important to be able to measure time. You might point out moments in class when measuring time is important; for example, when doing a science experiment or following a schedule.

Teaching Points

Write the letter *k* on the board, and invite children to make the sound. Ask children to look through the book for words that have the /k/ sound. Point out that not all words with the letter *k* will have this sound (*know*), and some words without the letter *k* will. Lead children to the various spellings of /k/: *k, c, ck,* and *ch.*

Review with children the long-vowel spelling pattern CVCe. Write the following words on the board for children to read aloud: *take, bake, time, game.* Ask children what they notice about these words, and confirm that they all end with a silent letter *e* and they all have a long-vowel sound. Let children replace the first letter of each to create new words with long-vowel sounds, such as *make, lake, rake; dime, lime, slime; lame, same.*

Reading and Writing Connections

Write the following sentence starters on the board for children to copy and complete: *It takes a short time to ___. It takes a long time to ___.* Ask children to think of two activities—one that can be done quickly and one that takes a longer time to complete. Tell children to write their ideas in each sentence and then exchange papers with a partner to read each other's ideas.

School-to-Home Connection

Invite children to take home their School-to-Home book to read with their families. Then encourage children to observe activities they and their families do at home and how much time they need for each. For example, how long does it take to prepare dinner? How long does it take to brush their teeth? Tell children to have family members time the activities. Let children compare times with the group.

Bibliography

Nonfiction

Older, Jules. *Telling Time.* Watertown, MA: Charlesbridge Publishing, 2000.

Fiction

Hindley, Judy. *Isn't It Time?* Cambridge, MA: Candlewick Press, 1996.

Murphy, Stuart J. *Game Time!* New York: HarperCollins, 2000.

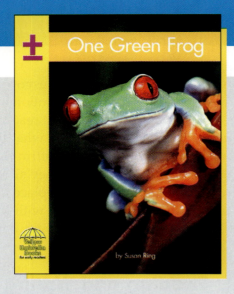

One Green Frog

by Susan Ring

–eet (*feet, sweet*), –ea (*eats, leaf, leaves*); long /o/ –ow (*grow, slowly*); final –y (*crunchy, many, very*); diphthong /ou/ (*count, ground*); /v/, initial (*very, vines*), medial (*leaves, lives, moves*); variant vowel /ô/ –aw (*claws, crawl*)

Supports

- Good photo/text support
- Interactive text
- Consistent print placement
- Predictable format: sentence followed by a question
- Repetitive language patterns: ___ *live in the rain forest, too. How many ___ do you see?*

Challenges

- Three sentences on pages 2, 7, and 8
- Various pronunciations of *or*: *forest/colors*
- Plural ending –ies: *berries, butterflies*
- Adjective ending –ly: *quickly, slowly*
- Distinction between verb ending –s (*eats, lives, moves, sits*) and plural ending –s (*ants, bats, birds, claws, colors, ears, flowers, frogs, hands, hummingbirds, mushrooms, petals, shapes, vines*)
- Concept vocabulary: *berries, butterflies, claws, crawl, crunchy, ears, hummingbirds, monkeys, mushrooms, petals, rain forest, sloth*

Standards and Benchmarks

See chart p. 89

Text Features

- **Word Count:** 215
- **High-Frequency Words:** *a, and, are, big, can, do, have, in, it, on, see, that, the, this, to, up, with, you*
- **Average Text Per Page:** 2-3 sentences, 12-17 words
- **Phonics/Word Study:** /m/, initial (*many, monkeys, moves, mushrooms*); initial *r*-blends *cr* (*crawl, crunchy*), *fr* (*frog*), *gr* (*green, ground, grow*), *tr* (*trees, treetops*); initial *l* blends *bl* (*blue*), *cl* (*claws*), *fl* (*flowers*), *sl* (*sloth, slowly*); long /e/ –ee (*see, trees, treetops*), –een (*green*),

 ## Preparing for Reading

Invite children to think about plants and animals that live in a natural habitat in their community, such as a local forest, pond, park, beach, swamp, or even backyard. Then encourage children to name other habitats. When someone suggests *rain forest*, write the words on the board. Speculate with children how the plants and animals in a rain forest might differ from those that live near them. Write the rain-forest animal names on the board, and read them with the group.

 ## Introducing the Book

Then display the book, and have children read the book title. Share with children that this frog lives in the rain forest. Now draw attention to the number word in the book title: *One*. Ask children how this number and the rain-forest animal might be used together in the book. Prepare children for the idea that they will be counting things found in a rain forest as they read.

 ## First Reading

Have children point to and read the book title and author's name on the title page. Ask them if the photograph shows "one green frog," and then encourage them to describe what it does show.

Turn to page 2, and ask children to read the first three words. Make sure they recognize these words as the book title. Repeat the question at the end of the page, and tell children to keep in mind the animals they named before reading.

For page 3, ask children to quietly study the picture for a moment, and then ask them to read the text. Point out that acknowledging the animals in the photograph as "blue frogs" prepared them for reading. Continue with page 4. Help children work through the first word on the page, making sure they understand that this bird is shown in the picture. After reading page 5, ask children what they notice about the format of the text, and help them realize that each page begins with a statement, and then asks a "how many" question. Explain that you do not want them to answer the question but to focus on reading the words. Have children finish reading the book.

Rereading

Have children explain what is special about this text. Help them conclude that this book not only tells them information, but it encourages them to participate by counting the plants and animals. Ask children if they enjoyed reading this book, and encourage them to read it again.

Discussing

Ask children if they think this book is a science book, a math book, or both. Encourage children to explain the parts of the book that make it science and that make it math. Then return to the beginning of the book and invite children to count the animals and plants. You might have children recall the names of each animal, and then read the question for them. Call on volunteers to answer, but make sure each child contributes. You might start a bar graph to record the numbers children count. Once all the animals and plants have been counted, you can review the bar graph to determine which animals or plants appeared the most or the least.

Teaching Points

Review with children that sometimes words that have the same sounds can have different spelling patterns. Write the words *sweet, feet*, and *eat* on the board, and have children say the words. Ask children which sounds are the same, and have them repeat *–eet* and *–eat*. Write these phonograms on the board for children to create new words. Explain that some words they create might be homonyms, like *meat* and *meet* or *beet* and *beat*. Other *–eet* and *–eat* words include *sheet*,

street, greet; heat, seat, wheat, cheat, treat, neat.

Continue your exploration of long /e/ by asking children to listen for other long /e/ words as you read the book. Tell them to raise their hands when they hear the sound, and write the word on the board. Ask volunteers to circle the letters that make the sound; for example, *ey* in monkey, *ie* in *berries*, and *ea* in *leaves*.

Reading and Writing Connections

Recall with children the animals and plants they named that live or grow in their community. Write the animal and plant names on the board, and assign one to each child. Challenge children to write two sentences about the animal or plant: one sentence to tell about it; and the other to ask the question *How many ___ do you see here?* Have children draw a scene with his or her animal or plant, and have children show their pictures and read their sentences aloud, asking group members to answer the question.

School-to-Home Connection

Invite children to take home their School-to-Home book to read with their families. Encourage them to look around their environment for items to count and to write sentences about what they see, modeled after those in the book; for example: *Teddy bears sit on my bed. How many teddy bears do you see?* Have them present the sentences to family members and work with them to answer the questions.

Bibliography

Fiction

Keats, Ezra Jack. *Over in the Meadow.* New York: The Penguin Group, 1999.

Murphy, Stuart J. *Every Buddy Counts.* New York: HarperCollins, 1999.

Saul, Carol P. *Barn Cat.* Boston, MA: Little, Brown and Company, 2001.

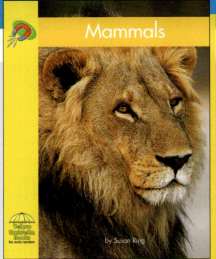

Mammals

by Susan Ring

Standards and Benchmarks

See chart p. 92

Text Features

- **Word Count:** 134
- **High-Frequency Words:** *a, also, and, are, can, for, have, her, in, is, of, on, or, some, the, their, them, they, this, to, too, will, you*
- **Average Text Per Page:** 1-2 sentences, 3-16 words
- **Phonics/Word Study:** initial consonants *b* (*baby, babies, bears, bison*), *h* (*hair, have, hot*), *m* (*mammals, many, milk, monkeys, mother*), short /e/ (*elephant,*

else); /k/, spelled *k* (*keeps, kind, kittens*), *c* (*can, care, cold, cool, cows*); /w/, spelled *w* (*warm, warm-blooded, weather*), *wh* (*whales*); medial digraph *th* (*mother, weather*); long /i/ –*ind* (*find, kind*); variant vowel /âr/ –*air* (*air, hair*), –*are* (*care*); silent *e* (*are, breathe, care, else, have, take, these, whales*); double consonants (*kittens, little, mammals, will*)

Supports

- Repetitive language pattern: _____ *are mammals*.
- Many short sentences
- Good photo/text support
- Consistent print placement

Challenges

- Question posed on pages 7 and 16
- Various pronunciations of *wh*: /w/ (*whales*), /h/ (*who*)
- Words with three syllables: *animals, elephant*
- Plural ending –*ies*: *baby, babies*
- Distinction between verb ending –*s* (*keeps*) and plural ending –*s* (*animals, bears, cows, dogs, kittens, mammals, monkeys, pigs, whales, years*)
- Concept vocabulary: *bears, bison, breathe, elephant, hair, mammals, monkeys, people, warm-blooded*

 Preparing for Reading

Show pictures of common mammals to the group, such as a cat, a dog, a deer, or a lion. As children study the pictures, challenge them to note what the animals have in common. Guide them to notice the animals' fur, as well as the fact that the animals need to breathe air. Then ask children this question: "Are these animals reptiles, mammals, or amphibians? How do you know?" Confirm that they are mammals, and encourage children to name other mammals they know. List their ideas on the board.

 Introducing the Book

Present the book to the group, and have children identify the animal on the cover. Ask, "How is this animal like the other animals we identified as mammals?" Children should point out the lion's fur and the fact that the lion breathes air. Then say the word *mammal*, inviting children to say the word with you. Ask children

which letters they hear in the word. Looking at the book title, ask children if they think this word could be *mammals*. Have them name the letters in the word and then read the word with you.

 First Reading

Ask children to identify the animal on the title page. You might have children say the sentence, "Wolves are mammals," preparing them for the repetitive language pattern of the book. With pages 2 and 3, make sure children can distinguish between *animals* and *mammals*. Help them notice the letters that differ.

Before children read each page, have them identify the animal in the photograph. Encourage them to find the word in the sentence, and then ask them to continue reading. For pages 10 and 11, ask children which activity the animals have in common. For pages 12 and 13, ask children what pigs and whales could have in common. With pages 14 and 15, let children have fun describing how the setting in each photograph is different. Ask, "What might this tell us about mammals?" Concluding with page 16, speculate with children how this photograph shows mammals. Invite them to read the page to find out.

Rereading

To help with one-to-one correspondence, write an animal name from the book on the board, such as *bear*. Have children read the word and then find the picture of the bear in the book. To further monitor comprehension, ask children to read the book again. Pause after several pages, and ask children to explain what they have just read.

Discussing

Point out to children that although mammals may look different, they all have some things in common. Challenge children to recall mammal characteristics from the book, and list their responses in a word web. Return to the list of mammals children named before reading. Ask children if all of the animals on the list are really mammals. Point out any animals that are not.

In addition, you could have children complete Venn diagrams for two mammals. In the outer circles, children would note what is unique about each mammal. In the intersecting circle, children would list characteristics they share as mammals.

Teaching Points

Write the word *mammal* on the board, and have a volunteer underline the repeated letters that appear together: *mm*. Ask children how these double letters are pronounced, and point out that they make the same sound as a single letter. Invite children to look through the book for other words with double consonants, such as *kitten*, *will*, and *little*. Start a list of words with double consonants for children to add to as they discover new words on their own.

For consonant review, assign one of these consonants to each child in the group: *b, h, m, k,* hard *c,*

and *w.* Have children use the book to find words that begin with their assigned letters and sounds, and have them write the words on a sheet of paper. Have children read their words to the group.

Reading and Writing Connections

Give each child four sheets of paper, stapled together to make a book. On the cover, have them write the word *Mammals*, along with their names. On the inside, ask children to draw pictures of animals that are mammals, one animal for each page. Encourage children to write the sentence ___ *are mammals.* below their pictures. In addition, you might encourage children to write additional sentences that tell extra information about mammals. Then invite children to read their mammal books to the group.

School-to-Home Connection

Invite children to take home their School-to-Home book to read with their families. Then encourage children to make one or two mammal puppets. Puppets can be made using craft sticks or brown paper lunch bags. When the puppets are complete, suggest that children and their families have a mini puppet play as they discuss the things that make mammals unique. In class, invite children to use their puppets to hold their own conversations about mammals.

Bibliography

Nonfiction

Heller, Ruth. *Animals Born Alive and Well.* New York: Penguin Putnam Books for Young Readers, 1999.

Kalman, Bobbie, Niki Walker, and Jacqueline Langille (editors). *What Is a Mammal?* New York: Crabtree Publishing Company, 1997.

Rabe, Tish and Lucille R. Penner. *Is a Camel a Mammal?* New York: Random House, 1998.

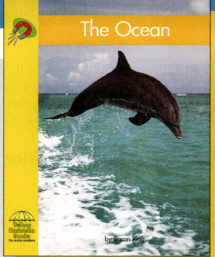

The Ocean
by Susan Ring

Standards and Benchmarks

See chart p. 92

Text Features

- **Word Count:** 139
- **High-Frequency Words:** *also, and, be, big, can, have, in, is, it, of, on, some, the, they, this, too, use, with, you*
- **Average Text Per Page:** 1-2 sentences, 5-15 words
- **Phonics/Word Study:** long /a/ –*ay* (*play, ways*), –*ale* (*whale*), –*ave* (*waves*); long /o/, spelled *o* (*also, cold, most, ocean*); long /e/ –*eef* (*reefs*), –*een* (*seen*), –*eep* (*deep*), –*eet* (*meets*); initial consonant blend *pl* (*places, plants, play*); ending consonant blend *st* (*forests, most*); ending –*y* (*many, salty, study, very*); variant vowel /ô/ –*al* (*also*), –*all* (*called*), –*alt* (*salty*); digraph *th* (*Earth, the*); /sh/, spelled *sh* (*fish*), *c* (*ocean*); /ch/, spelled *ch* (*beaches*), *tch* (*catch*); hard *c* and soft *c* (*called, calm, can, catch, coral, covered/places*); /f/, spelled *ph* (*dolphins*)

Supports

- Good photo/text support
- High-interest topic
- Draws on some prior knowledge
- Consistent print placement

Challenges

- No repetitive language
- Various pronunciations of *ea*: *beaches/Earth/ocean*
- Compound word: *underwater*
- Verb ending –*ed*: *called, covered*
- Distinction between verb ending –*s* (*grows, meets*) and plural ending –*s* (*animals, dolphins, forests, kinds, places, plants, reefs, waves, ways*)
- Concept vocabulary: *beaches, coral reefs, dolphins, fish, kelp, ocean, salty, underwater, waves*

 ## Preparing for Reading

Write the word *ocean* on the board, and read it for the group. Because several letter patterns have sounds that vary from rules children may have learned, children will need to be able to recognize this word as they read, rather than sounding it out. For example, the *c* in *ocean* does not have a soft or hard sound; it makes the /sh/ sound. And the spelling pattern *ea* does not make the long /e/ sound but rather a short /e/ sound. Practice saying the word with the group as you run your finger under the letters. Invite children to identify the sounds that the various letters or spelling patterns make.

 ## Introducing the Book

Present the book to the group, and invite children to find and read the word *ocean* on the book cover. Have them describe the cover photograph, identifying the image in the photo that is the ocean. Invite children to share information they know about the ocean, and list their contributions on the board. You might guide children's responses with such questions as, "Are oceans big or small? What lives in an ocean? Where can you see the ocean?" Record children's ideas to compare with the ideas in the book after reading.

 ## First Reading

Have children find and read the word *ocean* on the title page, and then discuss how the picture illustrates the ocean. Make sure children can reason that a sea star and coral are just some of the animals that live in the ocean.

Turn to pages 2 and 3. Have children compare the pictures. Ask, "What information might we learn about oceans on these pages?" Invite children to read the text, prompting them as necessary.

With pages 4 through 7, point out the repetitive phrase *in the ocean*. Challenge children to read the sentences, relying on clues in the pictures. Building on these reading strategies, work with children to read the rest of the book. You might explain that the sentences will not have a repeated pattern, but the pictures will help them figure out words and their meanings.

Rereading

Invite children to explain how the pictures may have helped them figure out new or unfamiliar words. Encourage children to turn to pages to share their strategies with other children in the group. Mention to children that reading a book a second time helps readers learn and recognize new words. It also helps readers to better understand what they have read. Invite children to read the book again.

Discussing

Review the information children knew about oceans before reading the book. Check off the information that was confirmed after reading. Then start a new list, encouraging children to call out the new things they learned about the ocean. Let children draw stars next to the new information that really surprised them.

You might also have children divide the book into subjects, suggesting chapter titles for certain sections. For example, pages 2 and 3 could be titled "What Is the Ocean?" Pages 4-7: "What Lives in the Ocean?" Pages 8-10: "Where in the Ocean Do Animals Live?" Pages 11-12: "What Is the Ocean Like?" And pages 13-16: "How Do People Use the Ocean?"

Teaching Points

Challenge children to find all the words in the book that have the letter *c*. Ask children to write down the words they find, and then share the words with the group. Help children group the words according to the sound made by the letter *c*; for example, the /s/ sound (*places*), the /k/ sound (*calm*), the /ch/ sound (*beaches*), and the /sh/ sound (*ocean*).

Have children turn to page 2 and locate the word *water*. Write the word on the board as children

say it. Then have them turn to page 4 and find a word that has the word *water* in it (*underwater*). Write this word on the board, too, and ask children what they think the word means. After accepting reasonable answers, point out that *underwater* is a compound word—a word made up of two words. Explain that they can figure out the meanings of compound words by thinking about the meaning of each individual word.

Reading and Writing Connections

Assign one of the ocean topics to each child in the group, such as ocean animals or how people use the ocean. Have children draw a picture for their topic, and then challenge them to write sentences that tell about the picture. Combine the pages into a group book about the ocean, and invite each child to read his or her page to the group.

School-to-Home Connection

Invite children to take home their School-to-Home book to read with their families. Then ask children to interview someone at home about his or her ocean experiences. You might have children write down questions to ask, such as, "What do you know about the ocean? Have you ever visited the ocean? What was it like?" Tell children to work with their families to write down the answers, and have children share their findings with the group.

Bibliography

Nonfiction

Berger, Melvin and Gilda. *What Makes an Ocean?* New York: Scholastic, Inc., 2001.

Denne, Ben. *First Encyclopedia of Seas and Oceans.* London, England: Usborne Publishing Company, 2002.

Simon, Seymour. *Oceans.* New York: William Morrow and Company, 1997.

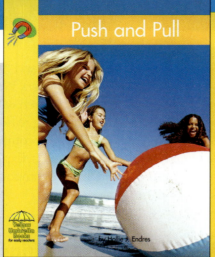

Push and Pull

by Hollie J. Endres

Standards and Benchmarks

See chart p. 92

Text Features

- **Word Count:** 184
- **High-Frequency Words:** *a, also, an, and, are, can, from, it, of, or, the, to, use, what, you, your*
- **Average Text Per Page:** 1-2 sentences, 5-19 words
- **Phonics/Word Study:** final double consonant *ll* (*ball, pull, roll*); digraph *th*, initial (*the*), medial (*another*), final (*both*); digraph *sh*, initial (*shut*), final (*push*); initial consonant blends *sl* (*sled, slide*), *sw* (*swing*); initial *a* (*about, another, away*); /ô/ with *r* –*oor* (*door*), –*orce* (*force*); diphthong /oi/ –*oy* (*toy*); long-vowel spelling pattern CVCe (*make, place, slide*); short /i/ (*swing*); short /o/ (*sock*); variant vowel /ô/ –*all* (*ball*), –*alk* (*talk*); variant vowel /är/ (*are, cart*)

Supports

- Repetitive language pattern: *You can _____ a _____ to make it _____.*
- Good photo/text support
- Familiar images
- Consistent print placement

Challenges

- Difficult science concept
- Questions on many pages
- Three lines on pages 4 and 10
- Various pronunciations of *ar*: *cart; toward*
- Concept vocabulary: *body, force, move, pull, push, roll, shut, slide*

 Preparing for Reading

Place an object on a table that can be pushed or pulled, such as a rope or a shoe box. Invite a volunteer to push the object, and then ask a second volunteer to pull the object. Ask children what happens when the object is pushed or pulled, and agree that the object moves. Have children say the words *push* and *pull* with you, and challenge them to help you spell the words. Write children's suggestions on the board, leading them to the correct spellings. Then ask children which other things they can think of that they can move by pushing or pulling.

 Introducing the Book

Display the book for the group, and encourage children to read the book title on their own. Looking at the cover photo, ask children what the people on the cover are doing—are they pulling or pushing? Continue questioning the group to help them understand the concept of push and pull. Questions could include: Why are they push-ing the beach ball? What will a little push do to the ball? What will a big push do? Instead of using their hands, how else could they push the ball? Nurture children's ideas to help them grasp the push-and-pull concept of movement.

 First Reading

After reading the book title on the title page, have children describe the movement used by the boy in the picture. Moving on to pages 2 and 3, have children first identify which picture shows a push (page 2) and which picture shows a pull (page 3). Then invite children to read the text.

As children read through the book, point out to them the repetitive language pattern: *You can [push or pull] a [object] to make it [movement].* Have children compare the sentence pattern as they study the sentences, side by side, on pages 6 and 7. Continue through the book in this way, encouraging children to study the pictures to come up with the correct words to complete the repetitive language pattern.

In addition, make sure children are able to distinguish between declarative sentences and questions. For example, on pages 12 and 13, ask children which sentences pose a question and have them explain how they know.

Rereading

Go through the book with the group, and have children identify the kind of force that creates the movement on each page. You might start a two-column chart, with one column for *Pull* and the other for *Push*. Have children suggest sentences for each column, such as, *You can pull a _____.* or *You can push a _____.* After reinforcing the terms and concepts, invite children to read the book back to you.

Discussing

Ask children to think about the things they moved that day. For example, did they pull their chairs out to sit down or push their chairs in after getting up? Did they pull off their coats or push up their sleeves? Let children have fun sharing ideas about all the things they pushed and pulled. Let children demonstrate pushing and pulling, encouraging them to express their ideas as they say the repetitive language pattern: "I [pulled] my [coat] to [take it off]."

Teaching Points

Invite children to say the word *push*, exaggerating the /sh/ sound. Point out that the /sh/ sound is often heard at the beginning of a word. Challenge children to think of words that have the /sh/ sound at the end, for example: *wash, cash, dish, fish, trash, mush,* and so on.

Write the words *door* and *force* on the board, and ask children to say them with you. Challenge children to say the sound that the words have in common—/ô/ with *r*. Then invite children to say other words with this sound. Start by having children substitute the initial consonant in *door* to make *floor*. Then lead children to learn other phonograms for this sound, including –*oar* (*roar, boar, soar*) and –*ore* (*chore, bore, shore, tore*).

Reading and Writing Connections

Assign children partners within the group. Ask each partner to draw a picture of something that is being pulled and another of something that is being pushed. Then have partners switch papers. Challenge children to write sentences for their partners' drawings that tell about the movement each drawing shows. You might write the repetitive language pattern on the board for children to copy and complete. Once the sentences have been written, ask children to switch papers again and to read the sentences their partners wrote.

School-to-Home Connection

Invite children to take home their School-to-Home book to read with their families. Then ask children to look around their homes for objects that are pushed or pulled to make them move. For example, children might notice that they pull and push a refrigerator door to make it open and close, or that they pull clothes out of a dryer and push clean clothes into a drawer. Have children draw pictures of pushing and pulling activities they do with their families, and challenge them to write sentences to go with their pictures. Have them share their ideas with the group the next day.

Bibliography

Nonfiction

Challoner, Jack. *Push and Pull.* New York: Raintree Publishers, 1996.

Murphy, Patricia J. *Push and Pull.* Scholastic Library Publishing, 2001.

Schaefer, Lola M. *Push and Pull.* Mankato, MN: Capstone Press, 2001.

Show Us Your Wings

Standards and Benchmarks

See chart p. 92

Text Features

- **Word Count:** 132
- **High-Frequency Word:** *a, also, an, are, at, can, do, has, have, in, is, it, on, some, their, they, this, to, too, us, use, with, your*
- **Average Text Per Page:** 1-2 sentences, 4-13 words
- **Phonics/Word Study:** /k/, spelled *ck* (*backwards, quickly*), *c* (*can, cannot, colors, insect*); /kw/, spelled *qu* (*quickly*); /gw/, spelled *gu* (*penguin*); silent conso-nant *k* (*know*); hard *g* and soft *g* (*penguins, wings/large*); long /o/ –*ow* (*know, show*); long /e/, spelled *y* (*heavy, ladybugs, many, only, quickly*); long /i/ –*y* (*butterfly, dragonfly, fly*); three-letter consonant blends *str* (*ostrich*), *spr* (*spread*); short /e/ –*e* (*help, insects, penguins, pretend*), –*ea* (*heavy, spread*); /ô/ with *r* –*oar* (*soar*), –*our* (*four, your*); double consonants (*butterfly, cannot, hidden, mammals*)

Supports

- Good photo/text support
- High-interest topic
- Draws on some prior knowledge
- Consistent print placement

Challenges

- No repetitive language pattern
- Compound words: *cannot, butterfly, dragonfly, ladybug*
- Various pronunciations: *ea* (*beats/heavy, spreads*), *ou* (*four/round*)
- Distinction between verb ending –*s* (*beats, spreads*) and plural ending –*s* (*animals, bats, colors, insects, mammals, penguins, spots, wings*)
- Concept vocabulary: *butterfly, dragonfly, ladybug, mammals, ostrich, penguins, soar, swim, wings*

Preparing for Reading

Invite children to pretend that they are flying. Most likely, children will flap their arms, imagining their arms as wings. Ask children to explain why they flapped their arms, guiding them to the word *wings*. Challenge children to help you spell the word, exaggerating each letter sound as children identify letters. Write the word on the board, and encourage children to share words that they associate with wings. Allow all reasonable responses, such as *fly, bird, airplane, feathers, sky, up and down*, and so on.

Introducing the Book

Show the book to the group, and invite children to find the word *wings* in the title. Read the entire title to them, and then ask them to point to the wings on the cover. Allow each child in the group to finger-trace the wings as he or she says the word *wings*. Then review the words children associated with wings. Discuss how these words are relevant to the book title and cover photo. For example, the picture shows a *bird*, the wings are covered with *feathers*, the wings look like they are moving *up and down*. Invite children to share any new words or ideas that the book title and cover inspire.

First Reading

Pause at the title page, and have children read the book title and finger-trace the wings in the photograph. Encourage children to describe the wings, noting how the wings shown here are different from the wings on the cover. (For example, they are transparent; they are not covered with feathers; they are on an insect, not a bird.)

As you explore pages 2 through 5, ask children to identify the type of animal in each picture. Make sure children recognize that the animals on pages 6 through 11 are insects, not birds. Before children read each page, encourage them to study the photograph to notice what is special about the wings. After finding the word *wings* in the text, invite them to read the sentence or sentences as best they can. Prompt children's reading as necessary, suggesting reading strategies.

Rereading

Some of the animal names in this book might be awkward for children to read. Write the words *dragonfly, butterfly, ladybug, penguin,* and *ostrich* on the board. Say each word, asking children to read and say the words with you. Then have children find the page that tells about each animal, using the photo for clues. Encourage children to find the word in the text, and then read the entire sentence with them. After reinforcing these words, let children read the book again.

Discussing

Have children call out animals from the book, and write the names on the board. Then ask children to explain what all these animals have in common, and confirm that these animals have wings. Challenge children to describe and explain what most wings help animals to do. Then ask children to name other animals they know that have wings. You might make animal sounds as prompts, such as *quack* for duck, *cock-a-doodle-do* for rooster, and *hoo-hoo* for owl.

Teaching Points

Write the word *wing* on the board. Cover up the letter *w*, and have children say the phonogram *–ing*. Encourage children to suggest letters to make new words with the phonogram *–ing*, such as *sing, ring, bring, fling, cling, zing,* or *sting*.

Ask children to turn to page 4 to find a word that begins with the letters *qu*. Point out that the letters *qu* make the /kw/ sound. Challenge children to come up with other words that might begin with *qu*. Write their ideas on the board, and let children check their ideas in a children's dictionary. Other *qu* words include *queen, quilt, quake, quiet,* and *question*.

Reading and Writing Connections

Assign to each child in the group one of the animals in the book. Ask children to draw their animal, and then to write a few sentences about the animal and its wings. You might suggest a few sentence starters, such as *I have wings. I ___ with my wings. My wings look like ___*. When ready, ask each child to "Show us your wings!" by reading the text but keeping the illustration hidden. Encourage the rest of the group to listen closely and to identify the animal based on their group member's description. Have the selected child reveal the photograph when the correct animal has been named.

School-to-Home Connection

Invite children to take home their School-to-Home book to read with their families. Then ask children to think about what it might be like to have wings and fly. How might they feel? What might they see? Where might they go? Encourage children to share their responses to these questions with their family members and then with the group.

Bibliography

Nonfiction

Miles, Elizabeth. *Animal Parts: Wings, Fins and Flippers.* Portsmouth, NH: Heinemann Library, 2002.

Singer, Marilyn. *Pair of Wings.* New York: Holiday House, Inc., 2001.

Fiction

Goodall, Jane. *The Eagle and the Wren.* New York: North-South Books, 2002.

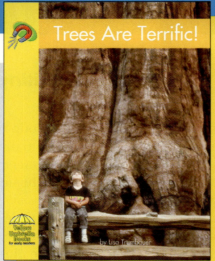

Trees Are Terrific!

by Lisa Trumbauer

Standards and Benchmarks

See chart p. 92

Text Features

- **Word Count:** 123
- **High-Frequency Words:** *and, are, big, from, have, in, is, it, of, no, some, that, the, too, will, with*
- **Average Text Per Page:** 1-2 sentences, 3-12 words
- **Phonics/Word Study:** initial consonant blends *fl* (*flat, flowers*), *pl* (*place, plant*), *br* (*branches*), *fr* (*from*), *gr* (*green, grow*), *tr* (*trees, trunk*), *st* (*stay, stem*); three-letter blend *spr* (*spring*); long /e/ –*ee* (*trees*), –*eed*

(*needles, seeds*), –*eave* (*leaves*); ending blend –*ld* (*hold, world*); hard *c* and soft *c* (*collect, cones, course, terrific/place*); digraph *ch* (*branches, change, which*); variant vowel /ô/ –*all* (*all, called, fall, tall*); variant vowel /ur/, spelled *er* (*evergreen, flowers, terrific, winter*), *or* (*color, world*); long /u/ –*ood* (*food*), –*oot* (*root*); CVCe spelling pattern (*cone, like, make*)

Supports

- Good photo/text support
- Familiar topic
- Draws on some prior knowledge
- Concepts build upon each other
- Consistent print placement

Challenges

- No repetitive language pattern
- Question on page 2
- Compound words: *evergreen, sunlight*
- Various pronunciations of *ow*: *flowers/grow*
- Irregular plural: *leaf, leaves*
- Plural endings: –*s* (*cones, evergreens, flowers, needles, roots, seeds, trees*), –*es* (*branches*)
- Concept vocabulary: *branch, cone, evergreen, flower, leaves, root, seed, sunlight, trunk*

 ## Preparing for Reading

Pass out art paper and crayons, and invite children to rely on their prior knowledge to each draw a picture of a tree. When finished, invite children to share their drawings. Have children identify features that their trees have in common, such as the leaves, the trunk, and, most likely, the colors brown and green. Let children write the words *tree, leaves,* and *trunk* on their drawings. Then ask children what else they know about trees. If possible, let children look through the classroom window to see trees around the school, prompting their ideas.

 ## Introducing the Book

Share the book with the group, and have children compare the photograph of the tree on the cover with their drawings. Ask, "What is the first thing you notice about this tree?" Have children describe the tree on the cover, and then ask them to find the word *Trees* in the book title. Ask them to explain why this word ends with the letter *s*, and compliment children on recognizing the plural form of *trees*. Then help them read the entire title. You might need to work through the word *Terrific*. Cover up part of the word, concentrating on isolated chunks, for example: *Ter-ri-fic*. Encourage children to define the word *terrific*, suggesting synonyms for this word, such as *great, fantastic, super,* or *awesome*.

 ## First Reading

Pause at the title page, and invite children to point to the book title and author. Make sure children can read the book title, praising them on recognizing *Terrific*. Briefly talk about the picture.

For pages 2 and 3, ask children to point to and identify the punctuation marks on both pages. Encourage children to explain the purpose of each, and then encourage them to use the correct phrasing as they read each sentence.

For pages 4 through 7, ask children to identify the plant parts they see in the photographs before reading. Invite the group to continue reading the book out loud. Children might not be familiar with the word *needles* on page 12. Write the long /e/ spelling pattern *ee* on the board, and ask children to say its sound. Add the letters *n* and *d* to the beginning and end, and have children read the word. Then remind them that the letters *le* make the /uhl/ sound. Adding the ending –*s*, ask children to put the sounds together.

Rereading

Have children point out facts in the book that they already knew about trees, such as the fact that leaves turn color in the fall. Then ask children to share with the group pages that held new information about trees. Ask the group to read the text on these pages. Then turn to the beginning of the book, and invite children to read again.

Discussing

Encourage children to think about trees in their community. Are there a lot of trees or just a few? Are there many different kinds of trees or are the trees very similar? Encourage children to consider why "trees are terrific" by pointing out some of the ways trees help us—for example, by giving us shade and helping clean the air. Invite children to think of their own reasons that trees are helpful to people, and write them on the board.

Teaching Points

Turn to page 6, and invite children to call out the plural words: *trees, branches, leaves*. Challenge children to tell the singular form of each word: *tree, branch, leaf*. Ask, "Which word was made plural by adding –*s*? By adding –*es*? By changing part of the word?"

Write the phonogram –*all* on the board. Ask children what they notice about this phonogram, and confirm that it is also its own word: *all*. Then

invite children to look through the book for other words with this phonogram. (*tall, fall, called*) Challenge children to create new words by replacing the initial consonant. Words children might make include *wall, stall, hall, ball,* or *mall*.

Reading and Writing Connections

Let children return to the tree drawings they made prior to reading. Ask children to write sentences that tell the new things they learned about trees. Tell children that they can use sentences from the book, but they should feel challenged to express their ideas in their own words. Invite children to share their sentences with the group.

School-to-Home Connection

Invite children to take home their School-to-Home book to read with their families. Then suggest that children take a stroll with a family member or older friend through their neighborhood to look at the trees. Instruct children to bring along paper and crayons to draw some of the trees they see. Back at home, ask children to write sentences to go with their drawings. Invite children to share their work with the group.

Bibliography

Nonfiction

Bulla, Clyde Robert. *A Tree Is a Plant*. New York: HarperCollins, 2001.

Hazen, Barbara Shook and Chiara Chevallier. *The Secret Life of Trees*. New York: DK Publishing, Inc., 1999.

Fiction

Locker, Thomas. *Sky Tree: Seeing Science Through Art*. New York: HarperCollins, 2001.

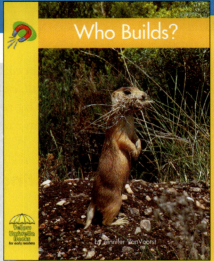

Who Builds?

by Jennifer VanVoorst

Standards and Benchmarks

See chart p. 92

Text Features

- **Word Count:** 97
- **High-Frequency Words:** *a, and, as, do, is, of, their, them, this, to, too, use, with, you*
- **Average Text Per Page:** 1-2 sentences, 3-14 words
- **Phonics/Word Study:** variant vowel /ur/, spelled *er* (*beavers, spiders, termites, together, towers*); variant vowel /ô/ –*all* (*tall*), –*aw* (*claws*); initial consonant

blends: *s* (*spiders, sticks*), *r* (*bridges, grass, tree*), *l* (*blades, claws, close*); final consonant blends –*ld* (*build*), –*lp* (*help*), –*nt* (*apartment*), –*st* (*nests*); digraph *th* (*their, them, these, things, this, together, with*); silent *e* (*blades, bridge, close, holes, live, termites, these, use*)

Supports

- Good photo/text support
- High-interest topic
- Encourages children to make connections
- Consistent print placement
- Repetitive language pattern: *People build ___. Animals build ___, too!*

Challenges

- Question on page 16
- Words with three syllables: *animals, apartments*
- Inflected word endings: –*es* (*bridges, houses*), –*le* (*people*), –*el* (*tunnels*)
- Plural endings: –*es* (*foxes*), –*s* (*animals, apartments, birds, blades, bridges, claws, dams, dens, houses, moles, nests, spiders, sticks, things, towers, tunnels*)
- Concept vocabulary: *apartments, bridges, build, dams, dens, houses, towers, tunnels, webs*

 ## Preparing for Reading

Display a set of building blocks or modeling clay, and speculate with the group what things they could build. If time allows, let children build with the blocks or clay, guiding their creations. Make suggestions for building houses, apartments, bridges, tunnels, towers, and dams. Discuss each building, and write the word for each on the board. Then ask children if they think animals build things, too, and why. Invite children to share what things animals might build, and write these words on the board as well.

 ## Introducing the Book

Share the book with the group, and encourage children to read the book title. Make sure children recognize the title as a question. Point to the animal on the cover, and ask, "Who builds?" Upon identifying the animal, let children have fun describing a home that this animal might build. Ask, "What materials might the animal

use? How can you tell? What other animal builders might we read about in this book?" List children's predictions on the board to check after reading.

 ## First Reading

At the title page, invite children to read the book title again, and encourage them to answer the question by identifying the animals in the picture. Have them also explain what the bees are building.

On pages 2 and 3, ask children if the pictures show animals or people. Have children find the words *people* or *animals* on each page to confirm their ideas, and encourage them to read each sentence.

After reading pages 4 and 5, and then pages 6 and 7, ask children what they notice. Make sure children recognize the repeated language: *People build ___. Animals build ___, too!* With pages 8 and

9, let children first figure out what the new word might be as they study the pictures. (*tunnels*) Have children sound out the word, and then find a word on pages 8 and 9 that has those letters. Repeat this process with pages 10 through 15. Conclude with page 16, inviting children to answer the question after they read it.

Rereading

Ask children which animal builders surprised them the most. Return to those pages, and invite children to find the name of each animal and the animal's building. When children have mastered these new words, encourage them to read the entire sentence or sentences. Let children read the book again from the beginning.

Discussing

Lead children to make comparisons between the structures that people build and the structures that animals build featured on each two-page spread. For example, on pages 6 and 7, have children explain how the "apartments" are alike and different. For pages 8 and 9, children could compare the uses of tunnels built by people and tunnels built by moles. You might record children's ideas on a two-column comparison chart. Read children's ideas back to them and challenge them to draw conclusions; for example: people and animals use the land around them to build; people and animals sometimes change the land around them to build.

Teaching Points

Say the word *build* slowly for the group, and challenge children to identify the three consonant sounds they hear: *b, l,* and *d*. Write the word on the board, and point out that the letters *l* and *d* appear at the end. They form an ending blend—two consonants that appear together, with each letter making its own distinctive sound. Encourage children to look through the book for other words with ending blends, such as *help* and *nest*. Tell children to say each word, exaggerating the consonants that make the ending blend sound.

Staying with the word *build*, ask children which two letters make the short /i/ sound. (*ui*) Invite children to look and listen for other words with the short /i/ sound in the book, such as *things, live, dig, bridges,* and *sticks.* Have them list the spelling patterns. (*i* and *ive*)

Reading and Writing Connections

Invite children to think of something they can build, perhaps referring them to the activity they tried before reading. Read the text on page 16 for children to answer, and then write these sentence starters on the board for children to copy and complete: *What can I build? I can build ____. I use ___ to build.* Challenge children to write one or two extra sentences to explain their building. Let children illustrate their ideas, too.

School-to-Home Connection

Invite children to take home their School-to-Home book to read with their families. Encourage children to work with their families to come up with other animal builders, suggesting that they consider animals in and around their homes. For example, perhaps they've seen anthills in the dirt or birds' nests in the trees. Invite children to write and illustrate a new two-page spread for the book; for example: *People dig holes for wells. My dog digs holes, too!* Invite children to share their work with the group.

Bibliography
Nonfiction

McDaniel, Melissa. *Busy Builders.* Tarrytown, NY: Marshall Cavendish, Inc., 2001.

Stewart, David C. *Animal Builders.* New York: Scholastic Library Publishing, 2001.

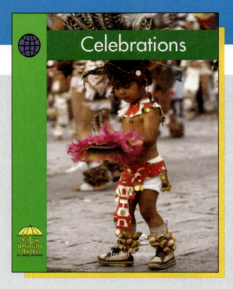

Celebrations

by Jeri Cipriano

Standards and Benchmarks

See chart p. 87

Text Features

- **Word Count:** 199
- **High-Frequency Words:** *a, all, and, do, for, give, in, is, it, of, that, the, their, they, to, what, you*
- **Average Text Per Page:** 2-3 sentences, 10-18 words
- **Phonics/Word Study:** hard *c* and soft *c* (*Cambodians, candles, Carnival, Cinco, colorful, costumes, countries, Mexican/celebrate, celebration, Cinco, dance, dancers, Independence*); initial consonant *j* (*Japan, Jewish, July*); long /o/ –*ow* (*glowing, grow, throw*); inflected word

endings –*le* (*candle, people*), –*al* (*petals, special*); digraph *th*, initial (*thanks, that, the, their, they, things, throw*), medial (*birthday, other*); long /u/ –*oon* (*moon*), –*oop* (*hoop*); diphthong /ou/, spelled *ou* (*around*), *ow* (*flower*); variant vowel /ur/, spelled *er* (*dancers, flower, lanterns, other, over, summer, winter*), or (*colorful, world*)

Supports

- Good photo/text support
- Encourages children to make personal connections
- Consistent print placement per spread
- One sentence on page 16
- Format follows the seasons in order

Challenges

- No repetitive language pattern
- Four lines of text on pages 4, 6, 14, and 15
- Compound words: *background, birthday, maypole, Thanksgiving*
- Various pronunciations: *ou* (*around/countries*), *ar* (*march/parades/carry*)
- Plural ending –*ies*: *countries, families*
- Many proper nouns
- Concept vocabulary: *background, birthday, candles, celebrate, costumes, dance, lanterns, masks, parades*

 Preparing for Reading

Ask children to recall the last holiday the class celebrated together. Write the name of the holiday on the board, and then elicit the ways in which the class celebrated. For example, did they make special foods? Complete a holiday art project? List these ideas on the board as well. Then encourage children to name other holidays they know. Once again, write children's responses on the board. Particularly guide children to holidays that are celebrated in other countries with which they might be familiar, such as Chinese New Year and Cinco de Mayo. Draw a star beside these international celebrations.

 Introducing the Book

Present the book to the group, and invite children to respond to the photograph. Speculate about what the child on the cover might be doing, as well as what he is wearing. Then help

children read the book title. Cover up most of the word, revealing small chunks at a time for children to master, such as: *Cel-e-bra-tions*. Discuss what *celebrations* means. Explain that in this book, children will discover different holidays or special days celebrated around the world. Have children predict which holidays they might read about, and check off those days on your list.

 First Reading

Have children read the table of contents on page 1. Ask, "How is this book organized? How do you know?" Make sure children recognize the names of the seasons as chapter titles.

Move on to pages 2 and 3. Ask children in which season the holidays on these pages occur, and have a volunteer point to and read the chapter title, "Fall." Before reading the text, ask children to point to words that begin with capital letters. Ask children to explain what is unusual about some of these words, and confirm that they appear in the middle of the sentence, not just at the beginning. Encourage children to explain why, and confirm that these words are proper nouns—they are the real names of holidays or cultures.

As children begin exploring each two-page spread, have them first find the proper nouns. Pronounce the words for the group. Praise children as they read each proper noun, assuring them that many of the other words in the text are not as difficult to read.

Rereading

Ask children which holidays in the book they think would be the most fun to celebrate. Have children turn to those pages, and encourage them to read the holiday and country or culture words. Then encourage children to read the book again.

Discussing

Invite the group to help you create a four-column chart to organize the information in the book. Title the columns *Season, Holiday, Culture,* and *How to Celebrate.* Work through the book with the group to complete the chart. For example, the information on page 2 could be organized in this way: *Season*—fall; *Holiday*—Carnival; *Culture*—West Indians; *How to Celebrate*—costumes, parades. When complete, discuss how organizing information in a chart is helpful.

Teaching Points

Invite children to copy words from the book that begin with capital letters. You might assign chapters to children to speed up the process. Tell children that some of the words will be proper nouns; others will be the first words of sentences. Invite children to read the words they find and to explain if the words are proper nouns or sentence beginnings. Explain that some words may be both, such as *Vietnamese* on page 3.

Write the words *country* and *family* on the board, and then challenge children to look through the book to find the plural form of each. Ask children what the words have in common. Explain that nouns that end with the letter *y* are made plural by changing the *y* to an *i* and adding *–es*. Have children think of other nouns that end in *y*, and help them practice making these words plural. For example: *puppy, lily, pony, party, story.*

Reading and Writing Connections

Encourage children to make invitations to a holiday celebration featured in the book. Write a few sentence starters on the board for children to copy, if needed, such as: *You are invited to celebrate ___. This holiday is celebrated by ___. We will ___.* Have children fold drawing paper in half to resemble a card on which to write their sentences. Let children illustrate their invitations, too, and exchange them with group members.

School-to-Home Connection

Invite children to take home their School-to-Home book to read with their families. Ask children to work with their families to create another page for the book, describing a holiday or special day that their family celebrates. Encourage children to work with their families to write sentences and illustrate the holiday. Have children share their family celebrations with the group.

Bibliography

Nonfiction

Chancellor, Deborah. *Holiday! Celebration Days Around the World.* New York: DK Publishing, 2000.

Jones, Lynda. *Kids Around the World Celebrate! The Best Feasts and Festivals from Many Lands.* New York: John Wiley and Sons, 1999.

Moehn, Heather. *World Holidays: A Watts Guide for Children.* New York: Scholastic Library Publishing, 2000.

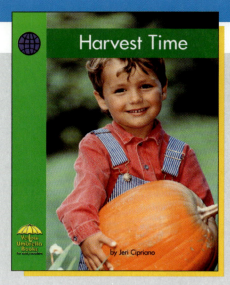

Harvest Time

by Jeri Cipriano

Yellow Umbrella Books
for early readers

Standards and Benchmarks

See chart p. 87

Text Features

- **Word Count:** 184
- **High-Frequency Words:** *a, and, are, be, can, from, in, is, it, of, on, the, they, this, to, too, up, uses, we, you*
- **Average Text Per Page:** 1-3 sentences, 9-18 words
- **Phonics/Word Study:** variant vowel /är/ (*are, garden, harvest, part*); inflected word endings *–le* (*apples*), *–el* (*kernel*), *–ed* (*harvested*); variant vowel /oo/ *–ook* (*look*), *–ould* (*would*); short /u/ (*cut, dug, pumpkin, up*); variant vowel /ô/ *–aw* (*strawberries*), *–alk* (*stalks*), *–all* (*called, tall*); /ô/ with r (*corn, orchard,*

sort); initial consonant *r* blends *fr* (*from*), *gr* (*grains, ground, grows*), *tr* (*tree*); digraphs *ch* (*orchard, reach, which*); three-letter blend *tch* (*patch*); long /i/, spelled CVCe (*time, vines*); variant vowel /ur/ (*kernel, ladder, under, worker*)

Supports

- Good photo/text support
- Draws on some prior knowledge
- Consistent print placement per spread
- Repetitive language pattern: *The ___ in the ___ are ready to be ___.*
- One or two sentences on most pages

Challenges

- Three sentences on pages 10, 12, and 13
- Words with three syllables: *harvested, potatoes, strawberries*
- Various pronunciations: *ea* (*ready/eat, reach, wheat, clean, peanuts*), *ou* (*ground/would*), *ar* (*are/orchard*), *or* (*worker/orchard*), *ch* (*orchard/machine*)
- Verb ending *–ed*: *called, picked, harvested*
- Plural endings: *–ies* (*strawberries*), *–es* (*potatoes*)
- Distinction between verb ending *–s* (*cuts, grows, sorts*) and plural ending *–s* (*apples, machines, peanuts, pumpkins, stalks, stems, vines*)
- Concept vocabulary: *field, grains, harvest, kernel, machine, patch, orchard, stem, stalk, vine*

 Preparing for Reading

Write the following words on the board, and encourage children to read: *apple, pumpkin, strawberry, potato, wheat, corn, peanut*. Review the words, and ask children what these objects have in common. Agree that these words are the names of foods. Also point out that each food is a plant—the food had to be grown before it could be eaten. Challenge children to identify which of the foods are fruits, vegetables, grains, and nuts, and list their ideas in a chart. Write the headings *Fruits, Vegetables, Grains,* and *Nuts* as well to familiarize children with these terms.

 Introducing the Book

Show the book to the group, and invite a volunteer to find the word on the board that identifies the object the boy is holding. Have

children look at the word *pumpkin* and determine if it is one of the words in the book title. Confirm that it is not, and then help them read the book title by isolating letter groups in *Harvest: Har-vest*. Ask children what they think the author means by "harvest time," and help children define the word *harvest*: the gathering of crops that are ripe, or ready to be eaten. Ask children if they think the pumpkin on the cover is ready to be eaten. How can they tell?

 First Reading

Have children explore the title page. Encourage them to recognize the words *fruits, vegetables, grains,* and *nuts* in the table of contents. Ask children how the word *harvest* has changed, and discuss how the letters *–ing* create a verb. Ask, "What does it mean to be harvesting fruits? How does this help us understand what we will read?"

Encourage children to identify the fruit on pages 2 and 3; then have a volunteer find this word on the board. Tell children to match the word on the board with the word in the book. Then invite children to read.

Continue with pages 4 and 5. Pause after reading, and ask children what they notice about the text. Make sure children begin to recognize the repeated language pattern: *The ___ in the ___ are ready to be ___.* Lead children to realize that the new words are 1) the food, 2) the place where the food grows, and 3) how the food is harvested. Encourage children to recognize and read the new words on their own, reminding them to look at the pictures if they have trouble.

 ## Rereading

Turn to pages 10, 12, and 13, which each have three sentences. Ask children to identify the beginning and ending of each sentence, showing you that they know sentence mechanics. Then invite children to read the book again to you. Listen for fluency and appropriate phrasing.

 ## Discussing

Ask children to contribute other foods they know to the four groups featured in the book: fruits, vegetables, grains, and nuts. Then talk with children about how the foods they suggested grow. For example, which foods grow on trees? (peaches, cashews, oranges) Which foods grow under the ground? (carrots, radishes, turnips) Which foods grow along the ground? (lettuce, broccoli, cucumbers) Which foods grow on bushes or other plants? (tomatoes, peppers, sunflower seeds) If a garden book is available, help children check their ideas.

 ## Teaching Points

Review with children the different ways that a word can be made plural. Have children turn to pages 2 and 3 in the book, and ask them to find the plural form of the word *strawberry*. Write it on the board, and ask children how *strawberry* was changed and made plural to

strawberries. Then write the word *potato* on the board, and ask children to find the plural form in the book (pages 6 and 7). Make sure children can identify the plural ending of this word as *–es*. Then ask children to look through the book for other plural words. Remind children that not all words that end with *–s* will be plural nouns; some may be verbs. Write the words children find, and discuss each to make sure children have correctly identified a plural noun.

 ## Reading and Writing Connections

Invite the group to create a "Harvest Time" mural. Let each child choose one of the foods from the book. Divide a length of mural paper so each child has a section to draw in, and then let children draw their foods, showing how the foods look when they are harvested. To complete the mural, have children write sentences that tell about their foods.

 ## School-to-Home Connection

Encourage children to share their School-to-Home book with their families. At home, ask children to have their family members help them create an advertisement that invites people to try a food that has been harvested. Suggest that they refer to a food they have at home for ideas. Then have children share their ads with the group.

Bibliography

Nonfiction

Saunders-Smith, Gail. *Fall Harvest.* Mankato, MN: Capstone Press, 1998.

Waters, Jennifer and Joan Stewart. *Harvest Time.* Minneapolis, MN: Compass Point Books, 2002.

Fiction

Gaines, Isabel. *Pooh's Fall Harvest.* New York: Random House, 2000.

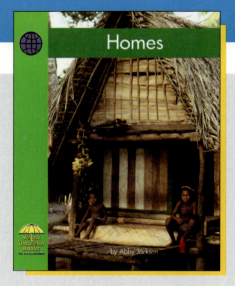

Homes

by Abby Jackson

Standards and Benchmarks

See chart p. 87

Text Features

- **Word Count:** 244
- **High-Frequency Words:** *a, all, and, are, at, but, can, do, from, go, in, is, it, of, not, some, the, their, they, this, to, us, we, with*
- **Average Text Per Page:** 2-3 sentences, 12-23 words
- **Phonics/Word Study:** /k/, spelled *ck* (*blocks, packed, pick, quickly, sticks*); initial *l* blends *bl* (*blankets, blocks*), *cl* (*clay*), *pl* (*place*); initial *s* blends *sl* (*sleep*), *sn* (*snow*), *st* (*stay, sticks, sturdy*); long /a/ –*ay* (*always, clay, day, stay*); long-vowel spelling pattern CVCe (*baked, made,* *make, place, safe, same; these; ice, inside, like; home, woven*); long /e/, spelled *ea* (*easy, eat, heat*), *ee* (*feel, keep, sleep*), *y* (*easy, everywhere, many, sturdy*); variant vowel /oo/ (*cook, look, wood*); long /u/ (*cool*); variant vowel /ur/, spelled *er* (*desert, different, shelter*), *ur* (*return, sturdy*); inflected ending –*le* (*simple, people*); short /a/ –*and* (*and, hand, sand*)

Supports

- Good photo/text support
- No more than three lines of text on most pages
- Encourages readers to make connections
- Consistent print placement per spread
- Repetitive language pattern: *This home is ___.*

Challenges

- Four lines of text on page 11
- Various pronunciations of *oo*: *cook, look, wood/cool, roof*
- Long-vowel spelling pattern CVCe with short-vowel sounds: *live, gives, some*
- Adjective ending –*ly*: *quickly, tightly*
- Plural ending –*es*: *branches*
- Distinction between verb ending –*s* (*gives, keeps, makes*) and plural ending –*s* (*blankets, blocks, homes, kinds, others, sticks, things, walls*)
- Concept vocabulary: *blankets, branches, build, clay, home, move, roof, shelter, simple, sturdy, wood, woven*

 ## Preparing for Reading

Share this riddle with the class: "I can be big or small, short or tall. I can be made of blankets or sticks, clay or bricks. What am I?" After children offer ideas, write the word *home* on the board. Repeat the riddle, and ask children what the riddle tells them. Confirm that homes can be any size or shape and be made of different things. Ask children to explain what all homes have in common, and write this main idea on the board: *Homes are places where people live.* (Due to privacy and sensitivity issues, do not press children to discuss their own homes.)

 ## Introducing the Book

Display the book for the group, and repeat the riddle. Ask children which detail in the riddle describes something about the house on the cover, and confirm that the house appears to be made of sticks. Speculate what this photo tells children about the homes they will see in the book. Agree that the homes will probably be made from different things, that they will probably be different shapes and sizes, and that they will probably be homes from around the world.

 ## First Reading

At the title page, invite children to read the book title, author name, and table of contents. Help children make predictions about the book based on the entries.

Ask children to read pages 2 and 3. Make sure they recognize that the chapter title is the same as the first sentence on page 2. After reading pages 4 and 5, have children compare the two homes as you say the last sentence: "But homes do not look the same everywhere."

Point out that this sentence prepares them for what they will read next.

Invite children to continue reading the book. Have them stop after page 10, and ask children if they notice a repeated language pattern. Moving on to page 11, have them point to the pattern here, too. As children reach page 12, ask how they think the homes in this chapter will be different from the homes in the previous chapter, and then have them finish reading.

Rereading

Ask children which home in the book surprised them the most, and encourage all children to turn to pages and offer ideas. Read these pages with the group, modeling appropriate fluency and phrasing. Then invite the group to turn to the beginning of the book and read it again.

Discussing

Have children recall the homes in the book, and then elicit conclusions they can make about homes. For example, homes are built to withstand the weather; homes reflect the environment in which they are built; homes are built with materials that are at hand, or available.

Talk about the various homes in the children's community. (Again, children do not need to discuss their own homes.) Does their community have mostly neighborhoods with separate homes? Apartment complexes? Rows of townhouses? Neighborhoods with trailers? Farmhouses with lots of land in between? List the homes on the board, and speculate with children why these homes are appropriate for the community. Invite children to help you write a new page for the book, choosing a home from their community and writing a few sentences about it.

Teaching Points

Write the word *cook* on the board, and invite children to say it with you. Erase the letter *k*, and write in the letter *l*. Ask children to say the new word, *cool*. Point out that although the vowels

stayed the same, they make a different sound. Ask children to look through the book for other words with *oo*. Ask volunteers to write the words under *cook* or *cool* to show how the word is pronounced. Work with children to come up with other words for *oo* and these pronunciations: *book, good, foot, took; food, spoon, tool.*

Reading and Writing Connections

Review with children the various homes in the book and the materials from which they are made. Then invite children to create their own fanciful, imaginative homes. Let children draw pictures of their homes first. Then have them write sentences modeled after those in the book. For example: *This home is made of ___. It is in ___. It has ___.* Encourage children to share their drawings and read their sentences to the group.

School-to-Home Connection

Invite children to take home their School-to-Home book to read with their families. Then invite children to choose one of the homes in the book that they found particularly unique or interesting, and challenge them to create a 3-D model of the home, using simple materials they have "at hand" at home. Encourage children to elicit help from family members. Suggest that children also write a few sentences about their models, explaining the materials they used. Ask children to bring their models to school to share with the group.

Bibliography
Nonfiction

Jeunesse, Gallimard and Claude Delafosse. *Houses.* New York: Scholastic, 1998.

Royston, Angela. *Where People Live.* New York: Raintree Publishers, 1998.

Schaefer, Lola M. *Homes ABC.* Portsmouth, NH: Heinemann Library, 2002.

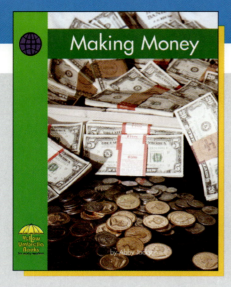

Making Money

by Abby Jackson

Standards and Benchmarks

See chart p. 87

Text Features

- **Word Count:** 234
- **High-Frequency Words:** *a, also, and, are, as, at, big, do, for, from, goes, has, in, into, is, not, of, that, the, their, them, there, they, to, too, use, was, we, with, you, your*
- **Average Text Per Page:** 2-3 sentences, 13-18 words
- **Phonics/Word Study:** /w/, spelled *w* (*want, was, we, workers, worn*), *wh* (*what, when*); medial digraph *th* (*clothing, other*); /ch/, spelled *ch* (*check, each, punched*), *t* (*pictures*); inflected word endings *–ed* (*printed*), *–en* (*taken*), *–es* (*pieces*); long /e/, spelled *ee* (*free, need, sheets*), *ey* (*money*), *y* (*ready, really, tiny, very*); long /a/ spelling pattern CVCe (*date, made, makes, mistakes, place, save, taken*); diphthong /oi/ *–oin* (*coins*), *–oy*

(*toys*); variant vowel /ô/ *–all* (*call, small*); /ô/ with *r* (*for, order, worn*); variant vowel /ur/, spelled *er* (*delivered, different, government, longer, order, other, paper, person, workers*), *or* (*workers*); double consonants (*bills, called, cotton, different, passed, really*); hard *c* and soft *c* (*call, called, circle, clothing, coins, cost, cotton, pictures; circle, pieces, place, replace*)

Supports

- Some photo/text support
- High-interest topic
- Draws on some prior knowledge
- Consistent print placement per spread
- One sentence on page 9

Challenges

- No repetitive language pattern
- Question on pages 7 and 16
- Four lines of text on pages 5 and 11
- Various pronunciations : *–ea* (*really/ready*), *–ear* (*earn/tear*), *–ost* (*most/cost*), *–or* (*workers/for, order, worn*)
- Verb ending *–ed*: *called, delivered, passed, punched, stamped*
- Distinction between verb ending *–s* (*gets, happens, marks*) and plural ending *–s* (*bags, banks, bills, circles, coins, jobs, machines, mistakes, pictures, pieces, things, times, toys, words, workers*)
- Concept vocabulary: *banks, coins, cotton, government, linen, metal, mint, money, punched, rare*

 ## Preparing for Reading

Hold up objects that children use every day and briefly talk about the materials from which each object is made; for example, crayons are made out of wax; pencils are made out of wood and lead; erasers are made out of rubber. Then hold up a dollar bill, and ask children what they think a dollar bill is made of. Is paper money really made of paper? What are coins made of? Elicit from children questions they have about what money is made of and how it is made, and write them on the chalkboard.

 ## Introducing the Book

Share the book with the group, and have children point to the paper money and coins on

the cover. Then read the title with them. Point out that this title could have two meanings, and challenge children to explain these ideas. One meaning could be how people earn money. The other meaning could be how money is actually created. Encourage children to share any ideas they have about how money is earned or produced. Then let children ask any questions they have about money. Start a KWL chart to record children's ideas.

 ## First Reading

Begin the reading with the title page. Have children read the title on their own, and then read with them the author's name and the entries in the table of contents.

Move on to pages 2 and 3. Because of the multiple lines of text on most pages, demonstrate how to track print and stay on line by placing a ruler or the edge of a sheet of paper below the line being read, then moving the ruler or paper to reveal the next line of text. Explain that this strategy will help them focus on one line at a time.

Invite individual children to read to you. Make sure children pause between sentences (at periods), as well as at commas. Let children mark particularly difficult words (like *government* on page 9) with sticky notes to review after reading.

 ## Rereading

Return to any difficult words children noted during reading. Offer strategies for reading the words. Have children read and repeat these troublesome words, and then ask children to read the book again to you.

 ## Discussing

Revisit the KWL chart you generated with the group before reading. Invite children to take turns reading what they knew about money, and what they wanted to know about money. Then ask children if their questions were answered. For example, did children learn what happens to old money? Did they learn what paper money is made from? Encourage children to help you complete the chart with new information they learned.

Finally, now that children have read the book, ask them to explain, in their own words, the two meanings that can be taken from the title, *Making Money.*

 ## Teaching Points

Work with children on the diphthong /oi/. Say the sound /oi/ for children to repeat. Ask children if they know which letters make this sound, and write the letters *oi* and *oy* on the board. Starting with *oy*, have children suggest consonants to create words, such as *toy, boy, joy,* or *soy.* Then challenge children to think of other words with this sound: *coin, join, noise, oink, joint,*

point, hoist, moist. Encourage children to identify the other letters that spell each word.

Read the book title with the group, and ask children which word was made by adding –*ing.* (*make*) Review that the letters –*ing* change an action word into the present tense.

 ## Reading and Writing Connections

Tell children that you would like them to help you write a new book, called, "The Penny in My Pocket." Have children suggest sentences that explain how the penny was made, how it arrived at a bank, and how it eventually ended up in someone's pocket. Write down sentences as children dictate them to you.

 ## School-to-Home Connection

Invite children to take home their School-to-Home book to read with their families. To reinforce concept vocabulary, suggest that children play a money memory game. Have them cut out 20 same-size rectangles, about the size of a dollar bill. On one side, tell children to write a word from the book, creating two cards for each word. Tell children to turn all the cards facedown, and then invite their families to turn over two cards at a time to read and find a matching pair.

Bibliography

Nonfiction

Hall, Margaret C. *Money.* Portsmouth, NH: Heinemann Library, 2001.

Otfinoski, Steven. *Coin Collecting for Kids.* Norwalk, CT: Innovative Kids, 2000.

Spies, Karen Bornemann. *Our Money.* Brookfield, CT: The Millbrook Press, 2001.

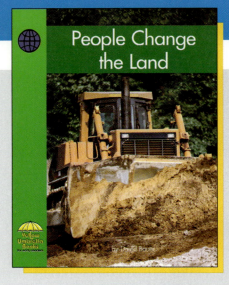

People Change the Land

by David Bauer

Standards and Benchmarks

See chart p. 87

Text Features

- **Word Count:** 222
- **High-Frequency Words:** : *a, all, and, are, can, do, give, go, in, is, let, of, some, that, the, they, this, to, too, us, use, was, you*
- **Average Text Per Page:** 1-2 sentences, 11-19 words
- **Phonics/Word Study:** short /i/, spelled *ui* (*build*); short /i/ –*ink* (*drink, think*); long /i/ spelling pattern CVCe (*alike, like, sides, sometimes*); /s/, spelled *c* (*cities, city, piece, place*); long /a/ –*ake* (*lakes, make*);

inflected word endings –*es* (*bridges, changes, houses*), –*le* (*people*), –*el* (*tunnels*), –*er* (*farmers, river, water*); diphthong /ou/, spelled *ou* (*houses, mountain*), *ow* (*how*); long /o/ –*ow* (*flow, grow*); variant vowel /är/ (*are, farmers, farms, garden*); /j/, spelled *dg* (*bridge*), *g* (*change*)

Supports

- Good photo/text support
- Draws on some prior knowledge
- Consistent print placement per spread
- Several pages with only one sentence
- Repetitive language pattern: *Before people change the land, a ___ might look like this.*

Challenges

- Text begins with three questions
- Four lines of text on pages 9, 10, and 14
- Various pronunciations: *oo* (*food, too/look*), *ou* (*mountain/through*)
- Plural endings: –*s* (*bridges, dams, farmers, farms, houses, lakes, tunnels, ways*), –*ies* (*cities*)
- Verb ending –*ing*: *building, digging, making, planting*
- Concept vocabulary: *city, bridge, build, dam, farm, lake, mountain, tunnel*

 Preparing for Reading

Invite children to help you create a simple picture of the community by asking them to name community features, such as streets, buildings, homes, and landmarks. The drawing need not be intricate, but should reflect the manmade and natural elements of the community. When the drawing is complete, ask children which features were created by people. As children watch, erase these people-made features, one by one, until only the natural elements of the community are left. Help children realize that once these people-made features are gone, only the land remains. Lead children to conclude that people changed the land when they built the community. Ask, "How else might people change the land?"

 Introducing the Book

Display the book for the group, and ask children to describe what the earthmover in the photograph is doing. Lead children to the phrase, "It is changing the land." Then direct their attention to the book title, and invite them to read it on their own. Predict with the group other ways that people could change the land, and record their ideas on the board.

 First Reading

At the title page, have children identify the title, the author's name, and the table of contents. Make sure children can also name the parts of the table of contents—the entries and the page numbers. Preview the book by reading the contents and comparing the ideas with predictions.

Invite children to read the text on pages 2 and 3, and then ask them to identify each place, using the words from the text. (*city* or *bridge* and *dam*) Review the other concept words with the group—*farm, tunnel,* and *lake.*

As children continue through the book, make sure they read the chapter titles. Also encourage children to note the sentences that are similar on pages 4, 8, 10, and 12: *Before people change the land, a ___ might look like this.* Explain that if children are not sure of a word, they should look to the photographs for information.

Rereading

Review concept vocabulary by having children pair a land feature with a human-made feature. For example: mountain—tunnel; river or lake—dam; land—farm or city. Then invite children to read the book back to you.

Discussing

Help children draw conclusions about the information in this book. Ask, "What do tunnels, bridges, cities, and farms have in common?" Make sure children can respond with, "These are ways that people change the land."

Then talk with children about why people change the land, and elicit ideas about the benefits of each change. For example, how are farms helpful? (They produce food.) How are cities helpful? (They provide places for people to live and work.) How are bridges and tunnels helpful? (They help people get from place to place more quickly.) How are dams and lakes helpful? (They provide people with drinking water.)

Teaching Points

Write the words *house, bridge,* and *change* on the board. Invite a volunteer to add the letter *s* to the end of each word, and have the group read the new words aloud. Ask children what they notice, and confirm that adding the *s* changes the word from one syllable to two syllables. Write other words on the board that will make this change, such as *horses, pledges, ages,* and *badges.* Have children clap the syllables for each.

Reinforce the pronunciations of words that have the same spelling but different sounds. Draw a Venn diagram on the board. Around the diagram, write the words *snow, cow, brow, bow, now, know, throw, how, wow, flow, grow, glow, low, chow, plow, stow, tow, vow.* Challenge children to pronounce each word correctly, sorting them into the separate outside circles of the diagram. For the intersecting circle, have children identify the word that can have either pronunciation—*bow*—and talk about the meaning of each.

Reading and Writing Connections

Elicit from children community features made by people, such as roads, bridges, farms, shops, and so on. Then ask each child to draw one feature and to write a sentence about it, completing this sentence starter: *People change the land when they ___.* Depending on the level of the group, you might let children write a few more sentences that explain how their chosen feature helps people. Then encourage children to read each other's ideas.

School-to-Home Connection

Invite children to take home their School-to-Home book to read with their families. Have children read the last page again and talk with their families about how they have changed or can change the land. Ask children to illustrate one of these instances, and then challenge them to write a few sentences to tell about it. Review children's work as a group.

Bibliography

Nonfiction

Hill, Lee Sullivan. *Dams Give Us Power.* Minneapolis, MN: Lerner Publishing Group, 1997.

Hunter, Ryan Ann. *Dig a Tunnel.* New York: Holiday House, 1999.

Johmann, Carol A. *Bridges! Amazing Structures to Design.* (Also in the series: *Skyscrapers!*) Charlotte, VT: Williamson Publishing Group, 1999.

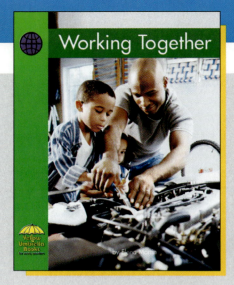

Working Together

Standards and Benchmarks

See chart p. 87

Text Features

- **Word Count:** 205
- **High-Frequency Words:** *a, all, are, be, big, boy, can, does, done, for, get, gets, girl, good, has, have, he, help, her, his, if, in, is, it, of, she, some, that, the, then, they, this, to, up, want, will, with*
- **Average Text Per Page:** 1-3 sentences, 10-21 words
- **Phonics/Word Study:** variant vowel /oo/ (*cook, good*); long /e/, spelled *ea* (*cleaning, each, leader, leaps, leaves, mean, team*); word ending –*er*/variant vowel /ur/, spelled *er* (*better, dancers, divers, firefighter, ladder, leader, member, others, together, workers*); variant vowel /ur/, spelled *er* (*different, person*), *ir* (*girl*), or (*work*); silent *e* (*are, dive, done, leaves, make, makes, more, safely, takes, these*); diphthong /ou/, spelled *ou* (*out, sound*); double consonants (*all, better, class, different, ladder, will*); digraphs *ch* (*coach, each*), *th* (*others, something, that, the, then, there, they, thing, this, together*)

Supports

- Good photo/text support
- Draws on prior knowledge
- Encourages reader to make connections
- Consistent print placement per spread
- Fewer than ten words on pages 2, 6, and 16

Challenges

- Very little repetitive text
- Four lines of text on pages 10 and 11
- Various pronunciations: *or* (*more/work*), *ou* (*trouble/out, sound*)
- Verb ending –*ing*: *building, cleaning, having, helping, working*
- Adjective endings: –*er* (*faster, safer*), –*ly* (*safely*)
- Distinction between verb ending –*s* (*gets, helps, holds, leaps, makes, takes, works*) and plural ending –*s* (*dancers, divers, ideas, jobs, others, workers*)
- Concept vocabulary: *better, building, cleaning, family, faster, leader, safely, team, together, work*

Preparing for Reading

Invite children to help you perform a simple task, such as repotting a classroom plant. Assign a different task to each child or to partners in the group, such as filling the new pot with soil, uprooting the plant, placing the plant in the new pot, filling a watering can, and watering the plant. When finished, ask children to describe what they have done. Write the words *working together* on the board, and ask children if they think these words could also describe the experience. Let children explain in their own words what it means to work together.

Introducing the Book

Present the book to the group, and challenge children to read the book title, matching it with the words you've written on the board. Have children speculate what the family on the book cover is doing and how the picture shows an example of working together. Then challenge children to think of other times when they might work together, or work with others. Lead children to some of the situations in the book, such as playing on a team, building a project, working with family members at home, and being part of a class. Encourage children to watch for their ideas as they read.

First Reading

Preview the book by discussing the title page. Ask children to explain how the people in the picture are working together. Then invite them to predict information by reading the table of contents. For example, "How are working together and working faster connected?" Record ideas to check after reading.

Invite children to read the first chapter on their own. Ask children if they noticed any repetitive language, and call attention to the sentence starter ___ *is a big job.* Encourage children to continue with the second chapter. Pause, and have children identify the people or workers in each picture. Before reading pages 10 and 11, have children identify the beginning and ending of each sentence to prepare them for reading these text-heavy pages. Moving on to pages 12 and 13, ask children how the text here differs from the text so far, and confirm that the sentences are questions. Then invite children to finish reading the book.

Rereading

As children read, you might have noticed moments that caused them to struggle. Review these pages with the group, helping children through pronunciation or phrasing challenges. Then invite the group to read the book back to you.

Discussing

Recall with the group situations in which the entire class or small groups worked together to create a project. Encourage children to explain the process. For example, did members work on different parts of the project? Were they able to learn from each other as they worked together? Invite the group to help you make a checklist of things they can do to make the "working together" experience go smoothly. For example: *We need to listen to each other. We can offer to help each other. We can each do a different job.* Let children suggest a place to display the list for the rest of the class to learn from.

Teaching Points

Write *fast* and *safe* on the board, and invite children to use each in a sentence. Point out to children that these words describe things. As children watch, add *–er* to each, creating *faster* and *safer.* (You might review that if the word ends with the letter *e,* they drop the *e* and then add the ending.) Say the beginnings of sentences for children to complete with each of these words. For example: *I can run fast, but you can run [faster]. One*

police officer makes the city safe, but two police officers make the city [safer]. Help children conclude that the letters *–er* change a describing word so it can compare two or more things. Let children try adding *–er* to other words, such as *tall, short, quick, slow, mean, nice, cold,* or *hot.*

Reading and Writing Connections

Challenge children to think of a big job they could do in school, at home, or in the community. Generate a list of ideas for children to choose from, such as cleaning a neighborhood park or planting a garden. Ask children to write sentences that tell how working together can make the job faster or safer or can help people do a better job. Jump-start their ideas by having them complete this sentence: ___ *is a big job!* Combine children's work into a group book for children to read on their own or to share with the group

School-to-Home Connection

Invite children to take home their School-to-Home book to read with their families. Then have children ask someone at home to help with a job. After completing the job, encourage children to illustrate the experience and write a few sentences about it. Ask children to read their work to the group and compare ideas.

Bibliography

Fiction

Bunnett, Rochelle. *Friends at School.* Long Island City, NY: Star Bright Books, 1996.

Falwell, Cathryn. *Feast for 10.* Boston, MA: Houghton Mifflin Company, 1995.

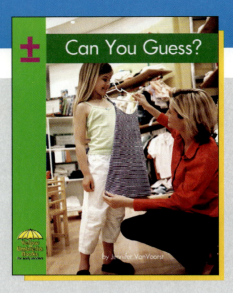

Can You Guess?

by Jennifer VanVoorst

Standards and Benchmarks

See chart p. 90

Text Features

- **Word Count:** 196
- **High-Frequency Words:** *a, also, an, and, are, be, by, can, comes, do, good, has, have, in, is, it, on, or, see, the, to, use, will, you, your*
- **Average Text Per Page:** 1-3 sentences, 8-23 words
- **Phonics/Word Study:** short /u/, spelled *u* (*bus, fun, lunch, much, sun, until*), *ou* (*enough*), *o* (*comes, stomach*); long /u/, spelled *ui* (*juice*), CVCe (*use*); long /e/, spelled *ee* (*feeling, need, see*), *y* (*every, exactly, many*); various pronunciations of *ch*: /ch/ (*lunch, much*), /sh/ (*machine*), /k/ (*stomach*); long /a/ *–ay* (*day, play*); /ô/ with *r*, spelled *or* (*or*), *ore* (*more*), *our* (*pour*); diphthong /ou/, spelled *ou* (*amount, count-*

ing, outside, without), *ow* (*growling, how*); /w/, spelled *wh* (*what, when*); double consonants (*glass, guess, setting, will*); silent letters (*answer, enough, know*); variant vowel /ur/, spelled *er* (*answer, longer, other, temperature*), *ure* (*measure, temperature*); long-vowel spelling pattern CVCe (*close, estimate, make, outside, plate, time, times, use*)

Supports

- Good photo/text support
- Draws on familiar experiences
- Consistent print placement per spread
- Only one line on page 12
- Only one sentence on pages 3, 5, 6, 12, and 13
- Some repetitive language: *Can you guess ___?*

Challenges

- Very little repetitive text
- Four lines of text on pages 7 and 15
- Words with multiple syllables: 3 (*cereal, estimate*), 4 (*temperature*)
- Various pronunciations of *ow*: *know/how*
- Adjective endings: *–ly* (*exactly*), *–er* (*longer*)
- Verb ending *–ing*: *counting, estimating, feeling, measuring, setting*
- Distinction between verb ending *–s* (*comes*) and plural ending *–s* (*gumballs, things, times*)
- Concept vocabulary: *amount, close, counting, estimate, exact, guess, measure, time*

 Preparing for Reading

Point to an object near the group, and say, "I think this desk is three feet long. What do you think?" Encourage children to suggest ideas, and write their guesses on the board. Explain to children that what you have asked them to do is to make a guess, or an estimate, of how long the desk is. Explain that estimating is quicker than measuring, but it is not as accurate. Then measure the desk (or other object) to see which estimate was the closest.

 Introducing the Book

Share the book with the group. Invite children to read the title with you, encouraging them to identify the title as a question. If children have difficulty with the word *guess*, cover up the letter *u* to direct their reading. Then ask children what the people on the cover are probably guessing. Agree that they are probably guessing, or estimating, if the dress will fit the girl, or the size of the dress. Speculate other everyday situations for which people might estimate, and list children's ideas to check after reading the book.

 First Reading

Encourage children to read the title on the title page, and then help them work through the words in the table of contents. Help them read *measuring, estimating,* and *amount.* Briefly talk about the picture, asking children what they could estimate. (the number of candies)

Ask children to read the chapter title and text on pages 2 and 3. Pause briefly, and ask children if these pages tell about estimating. Turning to pages 4 and 5, ask children to read the chapter heading, and ask if they will learn about estimating on these pages. Encourage children to read pages 4, 5, and 6 on their own. For the four lines on page 7, tell children to scan the text for words they know, as well as words that might be difficult. Then have them read the page to you.

As children read pages 8 through 11, point out the repeated language of the question, *Can you guess ___?* Have children continue reading, encouraging them to work through such concept vocabulary as *measure, guess,* and *estimate.*

Rereading

Mention to children that the text in this book is a mix of sentences that end with a period and sentences that end with a question mark. Challenge each child in the group to find an example of each and to read it aloud. Then ask all children to turn to the beginning of the book and read it again.

Discussing

Challenge children to explain in their own words what it means to guess or estimate a measurement. Then return to a page in the book that poses a question, such as page 9, 10, or 11. Encourage children to share their own experiences with guessing time or amounts, drawing ideas from the text and pictures. Then talk with children about when estimating can come in handy—for example, when they don't need an exact measurement, when they need to think of amounts quickly, or when they don't have a measuring tool.

Teaching Points

Say the following words, and ask children to listen closely: *count, amount, outside, without.* Challenge children to identify the sound that is the same, and have them repeat the sound /ou/. Then write the words on the board, and

have a volunteer circle the letters that make this sound. Add other words with this sound and spelling for children to pronounce, such as *sound, bound, hound, mound, fountain, mountain, counter,* and *pound.*

Extend the lesson to include the spelling pattern *ow* for the diphthong /ou/: *growling, how, fowl, now, cow, brown, town,* and so on.

Reading and Writing Connection

Tell children to each draw a picture of something that they can make an estimate about, such as an elephant (its weight or height), a jar of pennies (the amount), the sun (its temperature), and so on. Encourage children to be creative with their ideas. Then have children complete a question modeled after the one posed in the book; for example, *Can you guess how tall this elephant is?* Have children pass around their work for the rest of the group to read and discuss.

School-to-Home Connection

Invite children to take home their School-to-Home book to read with their families. Then have children discuss with family members the things the family estimates every day. Have children make a list, writing down their family's ideas. Then have children share and compare their lists with the group.

Bibliography

Nonfiction

Scott, Janine. *Take a Guess: A Look at Estimation.* Minneapolis, MN: Compass Point Books, 2003.

Fiction

Murphy, Stuart J. *Betcha!* New York: Harper-Collins, 1997.

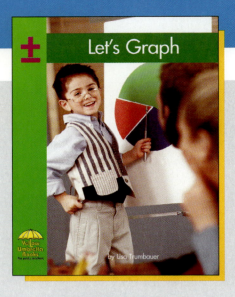

Let's Graph

by Lisa Trumbauer

final (*length*); /shun/, spelled *–tion* (*information, sections*); /ô/ with *r* (*information, more, shortest, sort*); long /o/, spelled *o* (*most, sold, total*); variant vowel /är/ (*bar, chart*); variant vowel /ô/ *–o* (*long*), *–ough* (*bought*); final double consonants (*class, sell, tell, will*)

Supports

- Good photo/text support
- Interactive text
- Consistent print placement per spread
- Only one sentence on page 15
- Some repetitive language: ___ ___ *have been sold. We can color in* ___ *bars on the graph.*

Challenges

- Words with multiple syllables: 3 (*chocolate, easier, understand*), 4 (*information*)
- Silent letters *gh*: *bought, doughnut*
- Various pronunciations: *ow* (*how/show*), *ee* (*keep/been*), *ea* (*learn/least*)
- Adjective ending *–est*: *longest, shortest*
- Distinction between verb ending *–s* (*helps, shows*) and plural ending *–s* (*bars, cookies, doughnuts, foods, graphs, pies, rows, sales, things*)
- Concept vocabulary: *bar graph, compare, count, pie chart, sections, sort*

Standards and Benchmarks

See chart p. 90

Text Features

- **Word Count:** 240
- **High-Frequency Words:** *a, and, at, can, do, has, have, help, in, is, of, on, or, that, the, they, this, to, us, use, was, we, were, will, you*
- **Average Text Per Page:** 2-3 sentences, 10-24 words
- **Phonics/Word Study:** short /a/ (*can, class, graph, having, track*); short /e/ *–ell* (*sell, tell*); /f/, spelled *ph* (*graph*); /k/, spelled *c* (*can, chocolate, circle, color, compare, cookies, count, picture, sections*); digraph *ch*, initial (*chart, chip, chocolate*), final (*each, much, which*); digraph *th*, initial (*that, the, they, things, think, this*),

 ## Preparing for Reading

Ahead of time, find examples of graphs in texts other than *Let's Graph*. Include a variety of sources, such as magazines, nonfiction books, math books, and so on. Pass around the samples for children to view briefly. Then ask children if they know what these illustrations are called, and write the word *Graph* on the board. Help identify parts of the graphs, such as the numbers and labels. Then speculate what graphs help people do. Explain that graphs help compare totals and amounts. The numbers are presented as an illustration to make comparing them easier.

 ## Introducing the Book

Show the book to the group, and invite children to find the word *graph* on the cover. You might review at this point that the letters *ph*

make the /f/ sound. Have children say the word with you, exaggerating the /f/ sound. Then ask a volunteer to point to the graph on the cover. Have the group compare this graph with a graph sample that you passed around. Point out the features that are the same, such as the numbers, labels, and captions. Tell children to look for these features as they read the book.

 ## First Reading

Open the book to the title page, and have children identify the book title, the author's name, and the table of contents. Review that a table of contents can help them preview a book, and then ask children which two types of graphs they will read about. (bar graphs and pie charts)

Because of the length of the text on pages 2 through 4, suggest that children first scan the text for words they know. Let children offer words they recognize, and write them on the board. Then ask children to read these pages out loud.

Continue this strategy as children move through the book. Invite individual children to read aloud to you, observing any words or passages that cause difficulty. Explain that you do not want children to study the graphs yet, but to concentrate on the text instead. As children read, make sure they include the chapter titles, too.

Rereading

Encourage children to suggest pages that they found hard to read or understand. Model reading these pages for the group. Then have children read those pages with you. Finally, ask children to read the book again.

Discussing

Talk with children about how the bar graph and the pie chart helped the children in the book learn about their bake sale. Make sure children recognize that a bar graph compares numbers. A pie chart compares parts of a total amount. Then work with the group to make a bar graph and a pie chart for objects in the room. For example, display a variety of books, asking children to sort them into such categories as poetry, fiction, and nonfiction. Guide children through the process of constructing each graph.

Teaching Points

Combine the use of bar graphs and pie charts with syllabication work. Ahead of time, choose a selection of words from the book with a variety of syllables. For example, *information* has four syllables; *easier, understand,* and *chocolate* have three syllables; *sections, compare, color, having,* and *cookies* have two syllables; *bake, class, graph, sold,* and *height* have one syllable.

Read the words to the group, and then ask children to say the words again as they clap and count the syllables. On a bar graph, have categories for one syllable, two syllables, three syllables, and

four syllables. Invite children to color in a bar for each word, showing the correct number of syllables. When all the words have been graphed, discuss which amount of syllables appears in the book the most and the least. Work with the group to create a pie chart, too, graphing the total amount of words discussed.

Reading and Writing Connections

Elicit ideas for other things children could compare on a bar graph, such as favorite flavors of ice cream or pizza toppings, favorite authors, birthday months, and so on. Assign a different topic to partners, and have them create a bar graph. Invite them to write a sentence or two about what their graph shows. Then invite partners to share their graphs with the group.

School-to-Home Connection

Invite children to take home their School-to-Home book to read with their families. Challenge children to think up a topic or object that they and their families could graph together, such as different coins in a piggy bank or different colors of socks or shirts. Invite children to graph the items, modeling the graph after one found in the book.

Bibliography

Nonfiction

Whitehead, Ann and Cindy Bickel. *Tiger Math: Learning to Graph from a Baby Tiger.* New York: Henry Holt Books for Young Readers, 2000.

Fiction

Bader, Bonnie. *Graphs.* New York: Penguin Putnam Books for Young Readers, 2003.

Murphy, Stuart J. *Lemonade for Sale.* New York: HarperCollins, 1997.

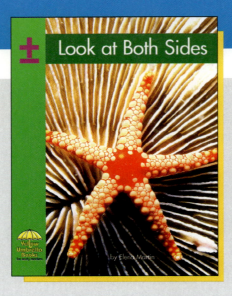

Look at Both Sides
by Elena Martin

Standards and Benchmarks

See chart p. 90

Text Features

- **Word Count:** 236
- **High-Frequency Words:** *a, also, an, and, as, at, but, can, for, has, have, its, no, not, on, see, that, the, they, this, to, we, you, your*
- **Average Text Per Page:** 2-4 sentences, 9-24 words
- **Phonics/Word Study:** short /i/ –*ing* (*things, wings*); long /i/, spelled CVCe (*kite, sides, sizes*), –*ight* (*right*), *i* (*kind*); long /a/, spelled CVCe (*face, same, shapes, snowflake*); long /o/ (*both, most, no*); short-vowel spelling pattern CVC (*dog, has, leg, not, rug, top*); final *y* (*body, symmetry*); variant vowel /ur/, spelled *er*

(*butterfly, different, pattern*), or (*colors*); diphthong /ou/ (*house*); double consonants (*bottom, butterfly, different, pattern, symmetry*); inflected word ending –*le* (*people*); final consonant blends –*ft* (*left*), –*nd* (*kind*), –*nt* (*different*), –*st* (*most*)

Supports

- Good photo/text support
- Interactive text
- Familiar images
- Consistent print placement per spread
- Several pages with only two lines of text
- Repetitive language patterns: *Look at ___ ___. This ___ has symmetry, too.*

Challenges

- Five lines on page 2
- Four sentences on pages 5 and 6
- Compound words: *butterfly, snowflake, sometimes*
- Words with three syllables: *butterfly, different, exactly, symmetry*
- Various pronunciations of *oo: look/too*
- Adjective ending –*ly: exactly*
- Distinction between verb ending –*s* (*looks*) and plural ending –*s* (*colors, shapes, sides, sizes, things*)
- Concept vocabulary: *both, bottom, exactly, left, look, right, same, shapes, sides, sizes, symmetry, top*

 Preparing for Reading

As children watch, draw a square, triangle, rectangle, and circle on the board. Have children identify each shape, and then draw a line down the middle that cuts the shape exactly in half. Challenge children to describe what they see on each side of the line. Then write the word *symmetry* on the board. Explain that when things have symmetry, one side looks the same as the other side. To further make your point, draw an unusual shape that would not have symmetry. Draw a line down its center, and ask children if the left side and the right side are the same. Explain that this shape is not symmetrical.

 Introducing the Book

Show the book to the group, and have children look at the book title. Ask them to compare the words in the title with the word *symmetry* that you've written the board. Challenge children to determine if the word *symmetry* appears in the title, and agree that it does not. Then encourage children to read the title on their own. Ask, "What does *Look at Both Sides* have to do with symmetry?" Mention that when we look for symmetry, we look at both sides of an object. Then ask children to look at both sides of the sea star on the cover. Ask, "Does this sea star have symmetry?"

 First Reading

Invite children to read the book title on the title page, and then ask them to identify other features, such as the author's name and the table of contents.

Model how to read the text on page 2 by covering up all but the first line with your hand. Tell children to focus on the first line of text. When they come to the end of the line, they should move their hands down to reveal the next line. Praise children when they reach the end of the page, making sure they know to move to the top of page 3.

Before children read page 4, have them read the chapter title, recognizing the word *symmetry*. On page 5, point out the line drawn down the center of the butterfly. Ask children what the line has to do with symmetry.

Have children continue reading the book. Tell them to look to the photographs for clues, but to concentrate on the text, not on answering the questions.

Rereading

Have children turn to pictures in the book that show examples of symmetry that they enjoyed. Invite children to read the text on their chosen pages. Then encourage children to read the book again from the beginning.

Discussing

Invite children to explain in their own words the idea of symmetry. Let children use examples from the book to explore their ideas. Pass out lengths of yarn, and demonstrate how to show the symmetry of items in the photographs that don't have a line down the center, such as on pages 8 and 9. Point out to children that if they could fold up the page, the two halves of each picture would match. Then invite children to look around the room and point out any objects or designs with symmetry.

Teaching Points

Review with children the short-vowel spelling pattern CVC. Write the words *has, not,* and *leg* on the board, and challenge children to describe how they are similar. Then ask children to look through the book for other words with short vowels and

this pattern, such as *rug, dog,* and *top.*

Write the word *symmetry* on the board, and ask a volunteer to circle the letter *y*. Have children say the sound each letter *y* makes, and help them hear that the first *y* makes the short /i/ sound, while the last *y* makes the long /e/ sound.

Reading and Writing Connections

Pass out drawing paper and have children fold the page in half to resemble a card. Encourage children to draw a shape on the card cover, using the fold line as one straight side of the shape. Explain that the shape can be something recognizable, like a house or a heart, or something abstract. Give children safety scissors, and have them cut out their shapes, not cutting the fold. Have children open their cutouts, and point out to them that their cutouts have symmetry; the fold line is the center line, and the shapes on each side of the line are the same. Invite children to write sentences about their cutouts to read to the group.

School-to-Home Connection

Invite children to take home their School-to-Home book to read with their families. Challenge children to create symmetrical shapes, following the directions above, with their families. Encourage children to create enough shapes to make a collage. Tell children to arrange their shapes in a pleasing design on darker, heavier paper, and then to glue them down. Let children share their symmetry collages in class.

Bibliography

Nonfiction

Kirby, David. *Patterns.* Barrington, IL: Rigby Education, 1996.

Fiction

Murphy, Stuart J. *Let's Fly a Kite.* New York: HarperCollins, 2000.

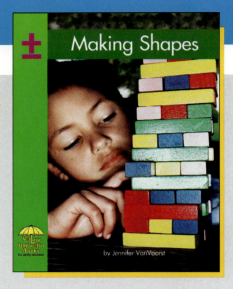

Making Shapes

by Jennifer VanVoorst

Standards and Benchmarks

See chart p. 90

Text Features

- **Word Count:** 254
- **High-Frequency Words:** *a, also, and, are, be, big, can, do, has, is, it, of, put, see, the, they, this, to, too, up, use, we, with*
- **Average Text Per Page:** 2-3 sentences, 11-25 words
- **Phonics/Word Study:** long /a/, spelled CVCe (*game, made, make, place, shape*), ay (*day, played*); long /i/, spelled CVCe (*inside, kite, like, slice, slices*); hard *c* and soft *c* (*can, circles/circles, slice, slices*); hard *g* and soft *g*

(*game, rectangles, triangles/bridge, orange*); inflected endings *–er* (*bigger, other, smaller, together*), *–es* (*slices*), *-le* (*circle, purple, rectangle, triangle*); variant vowel /ur/, spelled *ir* (*circle*), *ur* (*purple*); final digraph *ch* (*each, sandwich*); initial *l* blends *bl* (*black, blue*), *pl* (*place, played*), *sl* (*slice, slices*); short-vowel spelling pattern CVC (*big, can, fit, has, put, red*)

Supports

- Interactive text
- Similar shapes discussed per spread
- Consistent print placement per spread
- Only one sentence and nine words on page 3
- Some repetitive language: *You can make ___.*

Challenges

- Very little repetitive text
- Four lines of text on pages 4, 5, 6, 8, 10, 12, 14
- Words with three syllables: *everything, rectangles, triangles*
- Homonyms: *to, too, two*
- Adjective ending*–er*: *bigger, smaller*
- Verb ending *–ed*: *filled, played, shaped*
- Plural ending *–s*: *circles, shapes, slices, squares, triangles*
- Concept vocabulary: *build, circle, diamond, make, rectangle, shape, slices, square, triangle*

Preparing for Reading

Choose a classroom game that incorporates a variety of shapes, such as a board game, a card game, or a file-folder game. Display the game board or game cards, and challenge children to identify the shapes they see. Explain that the shapes can be the shape of the board or cards, shapes drawn on the board or cards, or shapes contained in images on the game. Invite children to finger-trace the shapes. Then elicit other places where children might see simple shapes. List classroom objects, such as the bulletin board, chalkboard, file cabinets, flags, pennants, and so on. Write the shape names on the board.

Introducing the Book

Display the book, and encourage children to identify the shapes they see on the cover. Tell children to not only consider the shapes of individual blocks, but the shape of the entire structure the child is making. Then say the word *shapes*, and challenge children to tell you how it is spelled. Have them look at the book cover and decide if a word in the title has this spelling. Then read the title with them. Speculate which other shapes children might see in the book, and write down their predictions.

First Reading

Open the book to the title page, and ask children to read the title. Have them also point to the table of contents and tell you how many chapters this book has. Encourage children to note how the chapter titles are similar to the book title. (They all begin with the word *making*.) Then review the shape names in the table of contents.

Have children preview the text on page 2 by scanning the text for the words *shape, squares, rectangles, triangles,* and *circles*. Have children read pages 2 and 3; then move on to pages 4 and 5. Suggest that children study the photographs to determine which shape they will read about, and then ask them to scan the text to find the word. Have them then read the pages.

Follow this reading strategy as children continue through the book: 1) Ask children to use the photographs to predict the shape; 2) Instruct children to scan the text to find the shape word; 3) Invite children to read the pages. Listen to children read, and suggest strategies if you observe children struggling. Challenge children to read the book in its entirety.

Rereading

Ask children if it helped them to scan the text for shape words before they read each pair of pages. Invite volunteers to demonstrate scanning for their classmates. Then ask children to read the book again, pointing out that the reading will go more smoothly the second time around.

Discussing

Turn to random pages in the book, and invite children to identify the shapes they see. After several pages, ask children why this book is called *Making Shapes*, and encourage them to summarize the book in their own words. Then call attention to objects around the room, and challenge children to "make shapes." For example, what shapes could they make if they put two books together? How about three books? Four books? What shapes could they make with pieces from the games they explored before reading? Help the group experiment with different objects and the shapes they can create.

Teaching Points

Write the words *triangle, rectangle, purple,* and *circle* on the board. Invite children to say these words with you, exaggerating the inflected ending *–le*. Have a volunteer come up to the board to circle the letters that make this sound. Then write and say other words with *–le*, asking the group to say them with you, such as *candle, huddle, tumble,* and *paddle.*

Ask children to find two describing words in the book that end with the suffix *–er*. Write the words on the board: *bigger, smaller.* Have a volunteer circle the root word of each: *big* and *small.* Have children notice how the words have changed to accommodate the suffix. Write other words on the board that need to have the last letter doubled, such as *hotter, fatter, redder, wetter,* and *madder.*

Reading and Writing Connections

Invite each member of the group to contribute to a "making shapes" collage. Have children cut out simple shapes from construction paper and combine them to form recognizable objects. Help children glue their shapes to mural or poster paper, leaving space near their shapes for their writing. Ask children to write a sentence that describes the objects they have made. Then invite the group to share their "making shapes" collage with the class.

School-to-Home Connection

Invite children to take home their School-to-Home book to read with their families. Then ask children to look through old magazines with their families for images created using a variety of simple shapes. Tell children to cut out the magazine pictures and glue them to construction paper, writing a caption about each. Review children's work as a group.

Bibliography

Nonfiction

Dodds, Dayle Anne. *The Shape of Things.* Cambridge, MA: Candlewick Press, 1996.

Fiction

Maccarone, Grace. *Three Pigs, One Wolf, and Seven Magic Shapes.* New York: Scholastic, 1997.

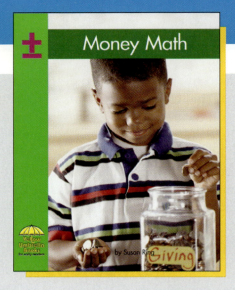

Money Math

by Susan Ring

Standards and Benchmarks

See chart p. 91

Text Features

- **Word Count:** 247
- **High-Frequency Words:** *a, also, and, do, does, has, have, he, is, it, my, she, that, they, this, too*
- **Average Text Per Page:** 3 sentences, 15-21 words
- **Phonics/Word Study:** short /u/, spelled *u* (*just, much*), *o* (*does, money*); short /e/, spelled *e* (*cent, else, penny, ten, twenty*), *ie* (*friend*); long /e/, spelled *ee* (*fifteen*), *ie* (*pennies*), *ey* (*money*), *y* (*fifty, forty, many, penny, thirty, twenty*); /s/, spelled *c* (*cent, cents*); /k/, spelled *c* (*coins*), *ck* (*nickel*); /kw/, spelled *qu* (*equals, quarter*); long-vowel spelling pattern CVCe (*dime,*

five, make, these); diphthong /ou/ (*found*); initial digraph *th* (*that, they, these, thirty, thirty-five, this*); /ô/ with *r*, spelled *or* (*forty*), *ore* (*more*), *ar* (*quarter*); double consonants (*different, pennies, penny*); ending blends *–nd* (*found, friend*), *–nt* (*cent, cents, different, twenty*)

Supports

- Sidebar with money and its number value
- Interactive text
- Concepts build upon each other
- Consistent print placement per spread
- Repetitive language pattern: *My friend has ____. How much money does he/she have? She/he has ____ cents.*

Challenges

- Number words: *one, five, ten, fifteen, twenty, twenty-five, thirty-five, forty, fifty*
- Words with three syllables: *different, together*
- The letters *ar* pronounced /ô/ with *r: quarter*
- Plural ending *–ies: pennies*
- Various pronunciations of *ie: friends/pennies*
- Distinction between verb ending *–s* (*equals*) and plural ending *–s* (*cents, coins, dimes, friends nickels, quarters*)
- Concept vocabulary: *cents, coins, different, dime, equals, money, nickel, penny, quarter*

 Preparing for Reading

Ahead of time, collect examples of pennies, nickels, dimes, and quarters to share with the group. In class, write the money values on the board: *1 cent, 5 cents, 10 cents, 25 cents.* Have children read the values with you. Then ask children which coins equal each money value. Write the words children suggest beside the correct amount: *penny, nickel, dime, quarter.* Then show children the money you have collected. Invite children to visit the collection, and ask them to show you which is the penny, the nickel, the dime, and the quarter. Pass the money around for children to feel and become familiar with.

Introducing the Book

Pass out the book to the group, and invite children to respond to the photograph. Ask chil-

dren what the boy is holding in his hand, and say the word *money* with the group. Have children look at the book title, and challenge them to identify which word is *money*, paying attention to the ending sound. Speculate with children what a book titled *Money Math* might be about, and list their predictions on the board.

 First Reading

Begin to explore the book by reading the title page. Ask children to quietly read the table of contents and then to tell you which words they read. Confirm that the words are the names of coins. Ask children why the words end with the letter *s.* (The words are plural.)

Talk with children about the format they see on pages 2 and 3: the chapter title, the position of the text, the photographs of the children, and the sidebar boxes with the coins and their values. Let children flip through the book, and help them notice that the book follows this format.

Then return to pages 2 and 3, and invite children to start reading. Encourage them to read as much of the text as they can on their own, guiding them only when needed. After children read pages 4 and 5, pause and talk about the repetitive pattern: the first sentence tells about a friend, the second sentence asks a "how much" question, and the final sentence answers the question. Have children read the book, focusing on the text rather than on answering the questions.

 ## Rereading

Review with children the money words and number words in the book. Call out words, and challenge children to find the page or pages on which that money or value is explored. Then ask children to return to the beginning of the book and read it again. Monitor the reading, noticing any words that still prove difficult.

 ## Discussing

Now that children have a firm grasp on the text, return to beginning of the book, and let children answer the "how much" questions. You might read the text to them, or let volunteers read aloud, encouraging the rest of the group to think about the answer. Once all the questions have been answered, ask children what this book helps them to do, and confirm that it helps them to add money. Turn to pages in the book, and invite volunteers to find the coins from the collection you brought to class to show the real-life example of the money on the page.

 ## Teaching Points

Review with children the /kw/ sound made by the letters *qu*. Ask children to find two words in the book with *qu*, and write the words on the board. Have children say the words, practicing the /kw/ sound. Then let the group look through a children's dictionary to find other examples of words with *qu*. Write the words children find,

and have children say the words with you..

 ## Reading and Writing Connections

Group children in pairs, and give each pair a set of random coins from your collection. Ask children to make combinations of coins and to create new pages for the book based on their combinations. Encourage children to write the money equations for each coin value, like the sidebars in the book, along with three sentences following the repetitive language pattern. Invite partners to read their work to the group.

 ## School-to-Home Connection

Invite children to take home their School-to-Home book to read with their families. Encourage children to identify small change family members have in their pockets, wallets, or change jars at home. With their families, challenge children to come up with new money combinations and equations. Tell children to write down their money equations to share with the group. They might leave the answer blank for groupmates to solve.

Bibliography

Nonfiction

Williams, Rozanne Lanczak. *The Coin Counting Book*. Watertown, MA: Charlesbridge Publishing, 2001.

Fiction

deRubertis, Barbara. *Deena's Lucky Penny*. New York: The Kane Press, 1999.

Murphy, Stuart J. *The Penny Pot: Counting Coins*. New York: HarperCollins, 1998.

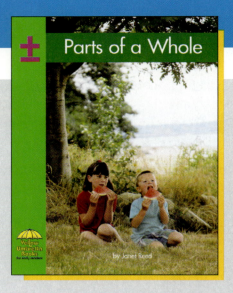

Parts of a Whole

by Janet Reed

same, size, slice, these, whole); silent l (half, should); /j/, spelled j (juice), g (orange); /ô/ with r, spelled or (orange), our (four, fourth); variant vowel /ur/, spelled ir (girl, third, thirds); /h/, spelled wh (whole); digraph th, initial (the, these, they, thing, third, thirds, this, three), final (fourth, with); digraph ch, initial (child), final (each, sandwich)

Supports

- Good photo/text support
- Draws on familiar experiences
- Consistent print placement per spread
- Some repetitive language: *You can eat a whole ___. When you eat ___.*

Challenges

- Mix of sentences and questions
- Four lines of text on pages 7, 8, 11, 15, and 16
- Irregular plural: *half/halves*
- Verb ending -ed: *called, divided, filled*
- Adjective endings: *–ly (exactly), –er (longer)*
- Distinction between verb ending *–s (wants)* and plural ending *–s (fourths, friends, parts, pears, thirds)*
- Concept vocabulary: *divided, equal, fourth, half, halves, parts, same, third, whole*

Standards and Benchmarks

See chart p. 91

Text Features

- **Word Count:** 252
- **High-Frequency Words:** *a, all, also, an, and, are, be, can, does, girl, have, in, into, is, of, or, the, this, up, wants, with, you*
- **Average Text Per Page:** 1-3 sentences, 11-24 words
- **Phonics/Word Study:** short /a/ (*apple, can, glass, half, halves, sandwich*); variant vowel /ô/ (*all, also, always, called*); variant vowel /är/ (*are, parts*); variant vowel /âr/ –are (*share*), –ear (*pear*); long /u/, spelled ui (*fruit, juice*); silent e (*are, divide, juice, make, orange,*

 Preparing for Reading

Hold up a sheet of paper, and say, "This is one whole sheet of paper. I am going to divide it into parts, one for each of you." As children watch, cut the paper in pieces, one for each group member and as close to the same size as possible. Give a piece to each child, and point out that they are each holding a part of the paper. Then ask a volunteer to collect the parts to make the paper whole again. Write the words *parts* and *whole* on the board, and read and say them with the group.

 Introducing the Book

Then present the book to the group, and explain that the words they've been practicing—*whole* and *parts*—are in the title. Have them read the book title, and then talk about the picture. Ask the group what the children on the cover are

eating. Ask, "Is a slice a *part* of a watermelon or a *whole* watermelon?" When children identify it as a part, invite them to consider other foods that they can eat in parts. For example, do they eat a whole pizza? Or a whole cake? List children's ideas on the board.

 First Reading

Now open the book to the title page, and have children recognize and read the book title again, as well as the name of the author. Direct their attention to the table of contents, and have children find the words *Whole, Wholes,* and *Parts.*

Before reading pages 2 and 3, have children point to the apple that is whole and the apple that is in parts. Have children scan the text for these words—*whole* and *parts.* Then invite children to read the text. Continue with pages 4 and 5.

Turning to pages 6 and 7, ask children what they think they will read about here, and help them read the chapter title. Before reading, have children identify the beginning and ending of each sentence. Then continue reading through page 9.

As children explore thirds and fourths, make sure they are able to make the connection between the numbers: thirds are three parts and fourths are four parts. Encourage children to find these number words in the text before reading. Then invite children to read the book to the end.

Rereading

Flip to pages in the book at random, and ask children if they see halves, thirds, fourths, or many parts. Write these words on the board to reinforce the concept vocabulary. Have children say the words several times with you. Then ask children to read the book again on their own.

Discussing

Remind children of the paper you cut into parts before reading. Ask children if any of the number words (*halves, thirds,* or *fourths*) applies to the number of parts you made. Share with children the new part word, if necessary, such as *fifths* or *sixths*. Then invite children to look around the classroom and name items in the classroom that could be divided into parts; encourage them to show how each item could be divided, and have them name the resulting parts as halves, thirds, or fourths. If the parts are fifths, sixths, etc. of a whole, help them to come up with the correct part name.

Teaching Points

Write the words *orange juice* on the board. Say the words slowly, exaggerating the /j/ sound. Ask children to identify the sound that the words have in common, and invite a volunteer to circle the letters that make the /j/ sound: *g* and *j*.

Then write the word *girl* on the board. Ask children how this word is like *orange*, and confirm that both words have the letter *g*. Have chil-

dren repeat the words *orange* and *girl* with you to hear the different sounds that the letter *g* can make. Then help children come up with other words for the hard *g* and soft *g* sounds, such as *game, gift, goofy, go; giraffe, gym, gem, germ.* You might introduce children to words that have both sounds, such as *garage* and *geography.*

Reading and Writing Connections

Write the following sentence starters on the board for children to copy and complete: *I can eat a whole ___. We can eat a whole ____ in ___.* Tell children to complete the first sentence with a food, and the second sentence with the same food and a "part" word. Tell children to draw a picture of their food as a whole and in parts. Then have children share their work with the group.

School-to-Home Connection

Invite children to take home their School-to-Home book to read with their families. Ask children to think of a simple snack they can make that uses whole foods or parts of foods. For example, half an apple covered with peanut butter. Encourage children to work with their families to write a simple recipe that uses ingredients both in whole amounts and in parts. Invite children to share their recipes with the group.

Bibliography

Nonfiction

Adler, David A. *Fraction Fun.* New York: Holiday House, 1997.

King, Andrew. *Making Fractions.* Brookfield, CT: The Millbrook Press, 1998.

Pallotta, Jerry. *Apple Fractions.* Scholastic, 2003.

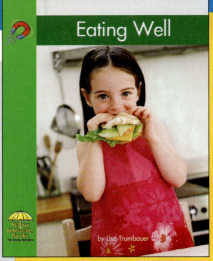

Eating Well

by Lisa Trumbauer

Standards and Benchmarks

See chart p. 93

Text Features

- **Word Count:** 214
- **High-Frequency Words:** *a, also, and, are, be, can, do, does, from, gives, have, in, into, is, it, not, off, on, or, the, to, too, what, with, you, your*
- **Average Text Per Page:** 1-3 sentences, 10-18 words
- **Phonics/Word Study:** long /e/ –*ean* (*beans, peanuts*), –*eat* (*eat, meat*), –*eed* (*need*), –*ese* (*cheese, these*), –*eeth* (*teeth*); long /a/ –*ay* (*day, may, stay*); digraph /ch/ (*cheese, chicken*); ending *y* (*body, dairy, energy, every,*

healthy, smoothly); long /u/, spelled –*oo* (*food, smoothly*); initial consonant blends *fr* (*from, fruit*), *gr* (*grain, group, grow*); initial consonant *y* (*yogurt, you, your*); *v*, initial (*vegetables, vitamins*), medial (*divided*), final (*five, give*); /k/, spelled *ck* (*chicken, kick, packed*); double consonants (*ball, eggs, different, soccer*)

Supports

- Good photo/text support
- Some repetitive text: *Which of these _____ do you like to eat?*
- Pages 2, 14, 15, and 16 only have one sentence
- Draws on prior knowledge
- Consistent print placement per spread

Challenges

- Three sentences on page 8
- Words with three syllables: *different, vegetables, vitamins*
- Irregular plural form: *teeth*
- Various pronunciations: –*ive* (*five/give*), *ou* (*fourth/group*), *ea* (*eat/healthy*)
- Distinction between verb ending –*s* (*gives, helps, needs*) and plural ending –*s* (*beans, bones, eggs, foods, fruits, groups, nuts, peanuts, vegetables, vitamins*)
- Concept vocabulary: *dairy, energy, fiber, fruits, grains, healthy, vegetables, vitamins, yogurt*

 ## Preparing for Reading

Share with children what you plan to eat for lunch that day. The night before, you might pack a lunch for yourself that includes foods from the food groups featured in the book: a grain, a fruit, a vegetable, a protein (such as meat or nuts), and a dairy food. Arrange the foods on a tray or paper plate, and encourage children to identify the foods. Then challenge children to name the foods in a more general way, and guide them to the food-group names. Write the group names on the board, and then list the foods from your lunch below them. For example: grain—bread; vegetable—tomato slice; meats, beans, or nuts—turkey; dairy—yogurt.

 ## Introducing the Book

Pass out the book to the group, and ask children to identify what the girl on the cover is

doing. (She is eating.) Write the word *eating* on the board, and then challenge children to read the book title. Discuss what the book title, *Eating Well*, means. List on the board the words children offer to explain the title, such as *healthy, good foods, proper diet,* and so on. Remind children of the lunch you brought to school. Ask, "Do you think that when I eat my lunch I will be eating well?" Have children explain their responses.

 ## First Reading

Open the book, and have children identify the book title, the author's name, and the table of contents. Review the purpose of the contents, and invite children to read the entries. Ask, "What will we read about on page 6? How do you know?"

Invite children to read the text on pages 2 and 3 out loud to you. Listen closely as they read, making sure children are able to track print properly and that they read with the correct phrasing.

As children read pages 4 through 13, ask them to first identify the foods in the picture on the right-hand page, and then have them read the food group in the heading on the left-hand page. Make sure children recognize the repeated question, *Which of these ___ do you like to eat?*

Finishing up with pages 14 through 16, ask children how the heading is similar to the book title.

Rereading

Turn to pages in the book and ask children to identify the foods in the picture. Challenge them to read the headings to confirm their ideas. Then invite children to read the book again to you.

Discussing

Talk with children about the foods in the lunch you shared with them before reading. Ask, "How is my lunch a good example of eating well?" Make sure children are able to recognize the five food groups, as well as the absence of anything sugary or "not healthy."

Then invite children to put together other lunch menus with healthy foods. Have children suggest foods for each group, and then have children mix and match the foods to make complete lunch menus.

Teaching Points

Write the words *grain, group,* and *grow* on the board. Have children say the words with you, and ask them which sounds and spelling pattern the words have in common. Invite volunteers to circle the consonant blend *gr* in each word. Then challenge children to come up with additional words with the *gr* blend, such as *great, grin, grill, grandmother, grunt, greasy, gross,* or *grip.*

Write the word *eat* on the board. Ask a volunteer to write the letter *m* at the beginning, and

have the group read the new word. Then ask which other words children can make, and list the words as they suggest consonants, such as *cheat, heat, treat, seat, wheat, neat,* or *beat.* You might point out that some words have two possible spellings for the same sound, such as *feat/feet, meat/meet,* and *beat/beet.* Challenge children to explain how the words differ in meaning.

Reading and Writing Connections

Write the following question on the board for children to copy onto a sheet of writing paper: *Which of these foods do you like to eat?* Then ask children to answer the question five times, each time listing a food from a different food group. Have children read their sentences out loud as you tally up the different foods to find the foods most children wrote about.

School-to-Home Connection

Invite children to take home their School-to-Home book to read with their families. Encourage children to work with someone at home to create a chart listing different foods for each food group. Have them take turns drawing and labeling foods for each column of the chart. Have children look through their kitchens, cookbooks, and magazines for ideas. Help children compare their charts in class.

Bibliography

Nonfiction

Haduch, Bill. *Food Rules! What You Munch, Its Punch, Its Crunch and Why Sometimes You Lose Your Lunch.* New York: Penguin Putnam Books for Young Readers, 2001.

Silverstein, Alvin, Virginia B. Silverstein, and Laura Silverstein Nunn. *Eat Your Vegetables! Drink Your Milk!* New York: Scholastic Library Publishing, 2000.

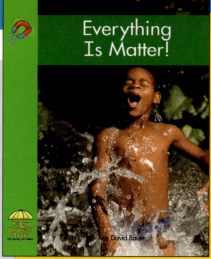

Everything Is Matter!

by David Bauer

Standards and Benchmarks

See chart p. 93

Text Features

- **Word Count:** 226
- **High-Frequency Words:** *a, and, are, but, can, do, gets, have, into, is, of, see, the, their, they, too, what, with, you*
- **Average Text Per Page:** 2-3 sentences, 8-19 words
- **Phonics/Word Study:** long /a/ *–ace* (*space*), *–ake* (*baked, make, take*), *–ape* (*shape*); initial consonant blends *br* (*breathe*), *fr* (*freezer, freezes, freshly*), *sm* (*smell, smelled*), *sp* (*space*), *st* (*start, steam*); hard *c* and soft *c* (*becomes, can, container, cookies, icicles/ice, icicles, space*); /w/, spelled *w* (*warm, water, weather*), *wh* (*what, where*); /sh/, initial (*shape*), medial (*freshly*);

th, initial (*the, their, they, things*), medial (*another, breathe, everything, weather*); variant vowel /ur/, spelled *er* (*another, container, ever, freezer, matter, water, weather*); hard *g* and soft *g* (*gas/change*); double consonants (*fill, happens, matter*); short /i/ (*liquid, solid*)

Supports

- Good photo/text support
- Some repetitive language: *Look around you. What _____ do you see?*
- Difficult science concepts build upon each other
- Draws on some prior knowledge
- Familiar images

Challenges

- Four lines on pages 3 and 10
- Multiple-syllable words: 3 (*another, container, definite, icicle*), 4 (*invisible*)
- Various pronunciations of *ea*: *weather/breathe, steam*
- Distinction between verb ending *–s* (*becomes, forms, freezes, happens, melts*) and plural ending *–s* (*icicles, liquids, solids, things*)
- Plural ending *–es*: *gases*
- Concept vocabulary: *container, gas, icicle, liquid, matter, shape, solid, space, steam*

 ## Preparing for Reading

Tell the group that you are going to write some words on the board. Ask children to read the words as you write them: *water, wood, stone, air, steam, juice, rain, ice.* Read the words with the group, inviting children to describe what the items are like. Share with children that all these objects have something in common, and write the word *matter* on the board. Have children say the word with you. Then invite a volunteer to look up the word in a children's dictionary. Depending on the reading level of the child, let him or her read the definition, too. (*Matter is anything that has weight and that takes up space.*) Briefly talk about how the objects you listed fit this category.

 ## Introducing the Book

Then share the book with the group. Have children identify the liquid (water) and the solids (the boy, the plants). Then ask children if they think air is present in this scene, and confirm that it is. Help children conclude, then, that everything in the picture is matter. Have children repeat the words *everything is matter* with you. Then call attention to the book title, and ask children to read it.

 ## First Reading

Introduce the title page and table of contents. Ask children to explain the purpose of a table of contents, guiding them with questions such as "What do the numbers tell us?" "What do the entry words tell us?" "How does someone use a table of contents?" "How is a table of contents helpful?"

Turning to page 2, have children match the heading and page number with the heading and page number in the table of contents. Then invite children to read the text. Ask children what they should read next, and have a volunteer move a finger from the bottom of page 2 to the top of page 3. Have them identify the beginning and ending of each sentence on page 3 and then read the text.

As children read the book, make sure they can distinguish between the chapter titles and the main text. Also monitor whether children are able to correctly track print from the bottom of one page to the top of the next. Help children through difficult words, such as *invisible* on page 9, by suggesting that they focus on small chunks: *in-vis-ib-le*.

Rereading

Choose pages that you noticed children had difficulty reading. Invite children to explain what proved challenging about the page. Was it the amount of text? Sentence breaks? Unfamiliar words? Encourage the group to read the page to you so the text becomes more familiar and easier to manage. Then have children turn to the beginning of the book and read it again.

Discussing

Ask children to share anything that surprised them in this book. For example, were they surprised to learn that air takes up space, even though they can't see it? Then play a guessing game using the categories solid, liquid, or gas. Have each child draw a picture that shows a solid, a liquid, or even a gas in a creative way. On the back side of the drawing, have each child write the name of the object, as well as its form of matter. Collect the drawings and show them one by one to the group, encouraging children to guess the name and form of matter written on the back.

Teaching Points

On index cards, write various two-, three-, and four-syllable words from the book. Ask children to help you sort the cards according to the number of syllables. Hold up each card, and ask children to read and say the word and then clap and count the syllables. List the words on a three-column chart: 2 syllables, 3 syllables, 4 syllables.

Reading and Writing Connections

Ask each child to draw a picture that includes a solid, a liquid, and a gas. Tell children to label the picture with sentences that identify the object and arrows that point to the object. For example: *The tree is a solid. The rain is a liquid. The air is a gas.* Invite children to share their drawings with the group.

School-to-Home Connection

Invite children to take home their School-to-Home book to read with their families. Then ask children to look through old magazines with a family member to find pictures of solids, liquids, and even gases. (Remind children that things that smell emit a gas, such as flowers, toothpaste, pizza, and so on.) Instruct children to cut out the pictures they like and to arrange the pictures into an "Everything Is Matter!" collage, grouping the pictures according to their matter. Review the collages in class.

Bibliography

Nonfiction

Cooper, Christopher. *Eyewitness Books: Matter.* New York: DK Publishing, 1999.

Robinson, Fay. *Solid, Liquid, or Gas?* New York: Scholastic Library Publishing, 1996.

Zoehfeld, Kathleen Weidner. *What Is the World Made Of? All About Solids, Liquids, and Gases.* New York: HarperCollins, 1998.

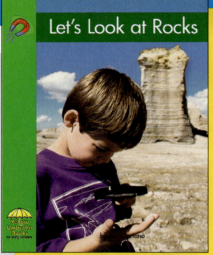

Let's Look at Rocks

hard *c* and soft *c* (*can, carve, cold, colors, cover/ice, once*); double consonants, medial (*called, different, fossils*), final (*all, wall*); inflected ending *–er* (*cover, river*); variant vowel /ur/, spelled *ear* (*Earth, learn*); variant vowel /är/ (*carve, hard, park*); long /a/ (*lakes, make*); variant vowel /ô/, spelled *al* (*all, called, chalk, chalkboard, walls*); diphthong /ou/ (*around, houses, mountains, out*)

Supports

- Good photo/text support
- High-interest topic
- Consistent print placement per spread

Challenges

- No repetitive language pattern
- Irregular past-tense verb: *make/made*
- Compound words: *chalkboard, classroom, everywhere*
- Opposites: *big/tiny; heat/cold; hard/soft*
- Plural ending *–s*: *animals, colors, figures, fossils, houses, lakes, mountains, plants, prints, rivers, rocks, statues, streets, tools, walls*
- Concept vocabulary: *beaches, chalk, chalkboard, fossils, mountains, jewelry, rocks, sand, statues*

Standards and Benchmarks

See chart p. 93

Text Features

- **Word Count:** 186
- **High-Frequency Words:** *all, and, are, at, big, can, do, have, in, is, of, on, or, see, the, them, they, to, too, us, use, you*
- **Average Text Per Page:** 1-3 sentences, 8-18 words
- **Phonics/Word Study:** initial consonant *r* (*rain, ran, rivers, rocks*); medial consonant *v* (*carve, cover, even, have, lived, rivers*); /sh/, initial (*shine, show*), final (*polish*); /k/, spelled *k* (*chalk, look, park*), *ck* (*rock*);

 ## Preparing for Reading

The night before the book is to be given to the group, collect a variety of rocks of different shapes, sizes, and colors, from a variety of locations. Distribute several rocks to each child in the group as you tell them about the different places the rocks were found. Then encourage them to share their rocks with one another, saying, "Let's look at rocks!" Ask children to describe their rocks to one another.

 ## Introducing the Book

Present the book to the group. Point to the book title, and encourage children to read it with you. Mention that the book title is the same as the sentence you said at the beginning of the session: *Let's Look at Rocks.* Have volunteers point to the rocks on the cover, and invite children to share what they know about rocks. You might guide their ideas with such questions as, "Why do you think there are so many kinds of rocks? What can you learn by studying rocks?"

 ## First Reading

Invite children to open the book to the title page. Have them identify the book title, the author's name, and the table of contents. Make sure children are able to identify the page numbers, as well as the chapter titles or entries.

Before turning to page 2, ask children which words they think they might see at the top of that page. Lead children to the first table-of-contents entry, *Rocks Everywhere*, and then turn the page to confirm their ideas. Point to the first sentence and ask, "Where have we seen these words before?" Make sure children can read and recognize this sentence as the book title.

As children read through the book, tell them to look for clues in the photographs that might help them read unfamiliar words. Then invite the entire group to read the words aloud to you.

Rereading

Return to passages children found difficult, and model them for the group, encouraging children to listen to you as you pronounce words correctly and apply appropriate phrasing. After you read, invite children to read the same sentence or page back to you. Then ask children to turn to the beginning of the book and read it again out loud.

Discussing

Ask children what they learned about rocks that they didn't know before. List children's responses on the board. Then with the group, consider areas around the school or community that children might not have thought of as rocky. For example, if children were surprised to learn that sand is rocks, help them recall the sandy shore at a beach or lake. If children were surprised to learn that mountains are rocks, recall a nearby mountain or rocky hill. List the community places next to each new fact you listed on the board.

Teaching Points

Review the /r/ sound with the group. Write the word *rocks* on the board, and have children say the word with you, emphasizing the /r/ sound. Then ask children to find other words in the book with the /r/ sound, such as *rivers, ran,* and *rain.* You might begin an /r/ word wall for students to contribute to as they discover other /r/ words on their own.

Also ask children to to look through the book for words that have the letter *c.* Ask children to sort the words acording to their sounds: /k/ (*can, cold*) and /s/ (*once, ice*). Challenge children to come up with additional words for each pronunciation of the letter *c.*

Reading and Writing Connections

On a sheet of writing paper, ask each child to copy the book title: *Let's Look at Rocks.* Then have children copy and complete this sentence starter several times: *A rock can be ____.* Encourage children to view the rocks you distributed to come up with ideas to complete the sentence. Let children compare their sentences.

School-to-Home Connection

Invite children to take home their School-to-Home book to read with their families. With their families, encourage children to think of places where they have seen different kinds of rocks. On poster board or the blank side of wrapping paper, have children work with their families to draw a poster, illustrating the different rocky places. The places can be as simple as a local park, a back yard, a nearby stream, a farm, a lake, and so on. Tell children to write captions for each place on the poster, too. Then review the posters in class.

Bibliography

Nonfiction

Gans, Roma. *Let's Go Rock Collecting.* New York: HarperCollins, 1997.

Ricciuti, Edward. *National Audobon Society First Field Guide to Rocks and Minerals.* New York: Scholastic, 1998.

Fiction

Spickert, Diane Nelson. *Earth Steps: A Rock's Journey Through Time.* Golden, CO: Fulcrum Publishing, 2000.

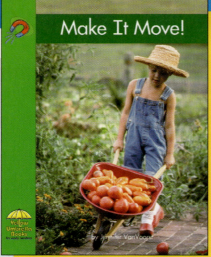

Make It Move!

by Jennifer VanVoorst

Yellow Umbrella Books for early readers

Standards and Benchmarks

See chart p. 93

Text Features

- **Word Count:** 215
- **High-Frequency Words:** *a, all, an, and, are, can, has, have, into, is, it, on, some, they, this, to, too, use, you*
- **Average Text Per Page:** 2-3 sentences, 12-23 words
- **Phonics/Word Study:** long /a/ (*cranes, plane*); variant vowel /âr/ *–air* (*stairs, wheelchair*); variant vowel /är/ (*are, parts*); inflected word endings *–le* (*axle, bottle, simple*), *–al* (*spirals*), *–es* (*wedges*); silent letter *k* (*knife*); /ks/, spelled *x* (*axe, axle*); /j/, spelled *j* (*objects*), *dg* (*wedges*); initial consonant blends *pl* (*plane*), *sl* (*slant, slide*), *sp* (*spirals*), *st* (*stairs*); medial consonant blend *cl* (*inclined*); three-letter consonant blend *scr* (*screw*); medial double consonants (*attached, bottle, pulley*); digraph *ch* (*attached, wheelchair*); /sh/, spelled *ch* (*machines*)

Supports

- Good photo/text support
- Recognizable objects
- Draws on some prior knowledge
- Consistent print placement per spread
- Repetitive language patterns: *A _____ is a simple machine. A _____ is a ___.*

Challenges

- Compound words: *everywhere, wheelbarrow, wheelchair, windmill*
- Various pronunciations: *–ine* (*machines/inclined*), *–ou* (*you/around*)
- Verb ending *–ed*: *attached, called*
- Distinction between verb ending *–s* (*makes*) and plural ending *–s* (*axles, cranes, levers, loads, machines, objects, parts, pulleys, spirals, stairs, things, wedges, wheels*)
- Concept vocabulary: *axle, inclined plane, lever, machine, pulley, screw, wedge, wheel*

 ## Preparing for Reading

Ahead of time, set up a quick display of simple machines that you have in class. Try to find examples from the book, such as a lightbulb, a jar lid, a plastic knife, a pulley, a bottle opener, and so on. Pass the objects around the group for children to study up close. Write *simple machines* on the board, and explain that simple devices, like those in the display, are called *simple machines*.

 ## Introducing the Book

Pass out the book to the group, and have children respond to the cover. Ask, "What is the child moving on the cover?" (vegetables) "What device, or simple machine, is the child using to move the vegetables?" (a wheelbarrow) Then challenge children to read the book title on their own. With the group, generate a list of devices, or simple machines, that children predict they might see in the book that help them move things or do an everyday job. Tell children to look for their ideas as they read the book.

 ## First Reading

Share with children that a table of contents can help them confirm predictions and make new ones about what they will read. Review the contents on page 1. Have children compare the listings on the contents page with their own list of simple machines. Explain that the words in the table of contents are general terms that describe many of the items that appear on the list.

Have children compare the photos on pages 2 and 3. Ask, "Which photo do you think shows a simple machine?" Encourage children to explain the difference between the simple machine and the machine shown in the other photo; then invite them to read the text.

Invite children to continue reading the book. Remind them that they should read the headings at the top of the pages, too. These headings let readers know what kind of simple machine they will read about. Stop the reading after page 7, and ask children if they notice a repetitive language pattern. Explain that the repeated pattern of *A _____ is a simple machine* and *A _____ is a _____* will help them read the book.

Rereading

Have children identify and read the heading on each page and then find the heading within the text. Make sure children recognize that these words are the general terms for each type of simple machine. Then invite children to read the book back to you.

Discussing

Review children's predictions about the simple machines they thought they might see in the book. Draw a star beside those machines that did appear. Then talk about how the other objects in the book are also simple machines. Turning to pages in the book, have children point to the simple machine and describe how it moves an object or helps people do work. You might record children's responses in a three-column chart. Have children notice that similar simple machines perform similar tasks. For example, a pulley lifts things; a wedge moves things apart or away from each other.

Teaching Points

Write the words *simple, bottle,* and *axle* on the board, and invite a volunteer to circle the letters that the words have in common. Write the letters *–le* on the board, and have children say the sound with you. Then say pairs of words, and invite children to distinguish which words end in *–le*, such as *window/candle; flower/double; bundle/bridges; puddle/weather.* Write children's

answers on the board and confirm words that end with *–le.*

Have children turn to page 13, and ask them to identify the object that has a simple machine. Write the word *wheelchair* on the board, and ask children why they think this is a good word for this object. Point out that *wheelchair* is made up of two words that tell about the object: *wheel* and *chair.* Indicate objects around the room that also have two words that tell about them, and write the compound words on the board— for example, *flowerpot, bookshelf,* and *chalkboard.*

Reading and Writing Connections

Have children write about the objects they explored before reading. Encourage them to modify the repeated language pattern of the book to tell about the objects; for example: *The car has a wheel and axle. A wheel and axle is a simple machine.* Let children draw the objects, and then write the sentences as captions.

School-to-Home Connection

Invite children to take home their School-to-Home book to read with their families. Give each child a list of simple machines from the book, and encourage children to work with their family members to find an example of each in their home.

Bibliography

Nonfiction

Fowler, Allan. *Simple Machines.* New York: Scholastic Library Publishing, 2001.

Hodge, Deborah and the Ontario Science Center. *Simple Machines.* Kids Can Press, 2000.

Nankivell-Aston, Sally and Dorothy Jackson. *Science Experiments with Simple Machines.* New York: Franklin Watts, a Division of Grolier Publishing, 2000.

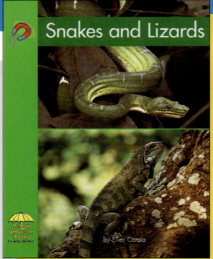

Snakes and Lizards
by Ellen Catala

Standards and Benchmarks

See chart p. 93

Text Features

- **Word Count:** 205
- **High-Frequency Words:** : *a, all, an, and, are, at, can, do, does, have, if, in, is, it, like, most, new, not, off, or, some, the, their, they, to, up, use, what, with, you*
- **Average Text Per Page:** 2-3 sentences, 9-23 words
- **Phonics/Word Study:** initial consonant blends *sc* (*scale, scaly*), *sk* (*skin*), *sm* (*small*), *sn* (*snakes*), *sp* (*special*), *br* (*breathe*), *gr* (*ground*), *pr* (*protects*); medial consonant blend *tr* (*control*); /k/, spelled *ck* (*backbone, flicks, picks, sock*); /sh/, spelled *sh* (*shade, shake,*

shed), *c* (*special*); long /i/ spelling pattern CVCe (*alike, reptiles, time*); long /a/ spelling pattern CVCe (*scale, shade, shake, snake*); long /e/, spelled *ee* (*feel, needs, peels, see*), *eal* (*meal*); ending *y* (*body, enemy, scaly*); diphthong /ou/ (*ground. mouth*); variant vowel /ir/–*ear* (*clear, ear, hear*)

Supports

- Good photo/text support
- High-interest topic
- Makes comparisons and contrasts
- Consistent print placement per spread

Challenges

- No repetitive language pattern
- Three sentences on pages 3, 7, 11, and 13
- Compound words: *backbone, cold-blooded, eyelids, underneath*
- Unusual letter pronunciations: *tongue*
- Various pronunciations of *ow*: *own/down*
- Word changes: *different/difference; body/bodies; scale/scaly; do/does*
- Distinction between verb ending –*s* (*flicks, knows, needs, peels, picks, protects*) and plural ending –*s* (*eyes, eyelids, legs, lizards, openings, reptiles, snakes, tongues, ways*)
- Concept vocabulary: *backbone, ears, eyelids, lizard, snake, shed, skin, reptile, tongue*

 ## Preparing for Reading

Divide the group in half. Ask one group to be the "snakes" and the other group to be the "lizards." Working together, ask children to draw pictures to show what their animals look like. When ready, help the groups compare their drawings. Guide their comparisons by asking such questions as, "What do lizards have that snakes don't? Which do you think is longer—a snake or a lizard? How do you think it would feel to touch a snake or a lizard?" Then ask, "What kind of animal are both snakes and lizards?" Write the word *reptile* on the board, and read it with the group.

 ## Introducing the Book

Share the book with the group, and invite children to read the book title as you point to each word. Invite a volunteer to point to and identify which animal on the cover is the snake

and which is the lizard. Have the rest of the group agree, challenging children to identify the physical features of each animal that helped them name the animal. Then ask children what questions they have about snakes and lizards, and list their questions on the board. Suggest that as children read the book, they look for the answers to some of their questions.

 ## First Reading

Briefly talk about the table of contents on page 1. Review its purpose, and read the entries. Based on these entries, have children predict if they think some of their questions might be answered.

Move on to pages 2 and 3. Have children first identify which is the snake and which is the lizard; then have them recognize and read the heading, *Reptiles*. As children read, listen for proper phrasing, especially with the series comma.

Pause after reading pages 4 through 7, and ask children if the information tells how snakes and lizards are similar or how they are different. (similar) Ask children to continue reading, this time looking for the ways the animals are different. Point to the headings, and explain that the headings will help them know what the information on each page will be about. As you monitor the reading, make sure children read the headings.

Rereading

Invite children to read the book back to you in their "snakes" and "lizards" groups. Have the groups (which might only be partners) take turns reading spreads. Encourage them to read the headings, too. Make sure children are able to move from the bottom of one page to the top of the next.

Discussing

Draw a Venn diagram on the board, and explain its purpose to the group—to help compare how two things are alike and how they are different. Write *Snakes* above one outer circle and *Lizards* above the other. Write the word *Reptiles* above the intersecting center circle. Encourage children to help you fill in the information they learned from the book about how snakes and lizards have similarities as reptiles and differences as individual species. For example, they are both cold-blooded; lizards have legs, but snakes do not; lizards shed their skin in pieces while snakes shed in one long piece; and so on.

Teaching Points

Write the words *snake, shade, scale,* and *shake* on the board, and encourage children to explain what the words have in common. Confirm that they all have the long /a/ sound, spelled with the silent *e*. In addition, the first two letters are consonant blends or digraphs. Work with children to come up with other words that follow this spelling pattern, such as *stake, brake, flake; shame, shape, Shane; stale; slate, crate.*

Reading and Writing Connections

Assign children partners, and invite one partner to role-play being a snake and the other a lizard. Encourage partners to write a short script for a conversation that a lizard and a snake might have that tells how they are alike and how they are different. Suggest that children look through the book for ideas, as well as for ways to draft their sentences. When ready, invite partners to read their scripts to the group as they role-play their animal parts. Depending on the level of the group, children could perform the role-play first as you tape-record the words. Then help children write the words from the tape.

School-to-Home Connection

Invite children to take home their School-to-Home book to read with their families. Encourage children to work with their families to create puppets for either a snake or a lizard. With their completed puppets, have children tell their families what is special about that animal. Invite children to share their puppets with the group.

Bibliography

Nonfiction

Bell, Simon M. and Dennis Bockus. *Snakes and Lizards: Eye to Eye Books.* London, England: Ladybird Books, 1997.

Berger, Melvin and Gilda. *Can Snakes Crawl Backward? Questions and Answers About Reptiles.* New York: Scholastic, Inc., 2002.

Spilsbury, Louise and Richard. *Classifying Reptiles.* Portsmouth, NH: Heinemann Library, 2003.

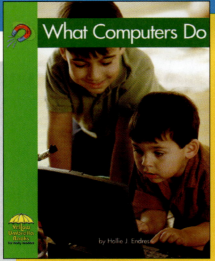

What Computers Do

by Hollie J. Endres

Standards and Benchmarks

See chart p. 93

Text Features

- **Word Count:** 186
- **High-Frequency Words:** *a, and, are, but, can, do, for, from, go, have, help, in, of, see, than, that, the, them, their, they, to, too, use, with, you*
- **Average Text Per Page:** 1-3 sentences, 8-16 words
- **Phonics/Word Study:** short /e/ (*sell, tell*); long /a/, spelled *ay* (*day, today*), CVCe (*games, make*); long /e/ —*ee* (*keep, see*); variant vowel /ur/, spelled *or* (*factory, work*); /ô/ with r (*for, information, sort, store*); /ch/, spelled *ch* (*teacher, much*), *t* (*picture*); /sh/ —*ch* (*machines*), —*tion* (*information*); digraph *th* (*another,*

math, together, with, without); double consonants, medial (*connected, letter*), final (*sell, tell*); inflected ending —*er* (*another, computer, faster, letter, owners, teachers, together, workers*); *v* (*have, microwave, oven, video*); ending blends —*ld* (*hold*), —*lp* (*help*), —*nd* (*send*), —*nt* (*student*)

Supports

- Good photo/text support
- High-interest topic
- Draws on some prior knowledge
- Consistent print placement per spread
- Some repetitive text: _____ *use computers.*

Challenges

- Words with multiple syllables: 3 (*another, computer, connected, everything, everywhere, factory, microwave, together, video*), 4 (*information*)
- Various pronunciations: *or* (*work/sort*), *ea* (*teacher/learn*), *ow* (*how/own*), *ave* (*have/microwave*)
- Long /i/ spelling pattern —*ine*, long /e/ sound: *machine*
- Verb endings: —*ing* (*leaving*), —*ed* (*connected, mailed*)
- Plural ending —*s*: *cars, computers, games, ovens, owners, pictures, pilots, scientists, students, teachers, things*
- Concept vocabulary: *computers, factory workers, information, machines, math problems, pilots, scientists, students, teachers*

 Preparing for Reading

As children watch, begin to draw a simple outline of a conventional personal computer with monitor on the board. Encourage children to jump in and guess what you are drawing when they think they know. When children respond correctly with *computer*, write the word *computer* above your drawing. Finish your drawing, making sure you have created a large screen in which you can write. Then ask children what they know about computers, and list key words within your computer screen. Lead children to words they will encounter in the book, such as *information, letter, teacher,* and *machine*.

 Introducing the Book

Share the book with the group, and talk about the cover photo. Make sure children can point to and identify the computer, and then have children find and read the word *Computers* in the book title. Rephrase the title as a question: "What do computers do?" Speculate why people use computers, as well as who uses them, and begin a two-column chart to list ideas: *Who Uses Computers?* and *Why Do They Use Computers?* Guide children to name people they will read about in the book, such as teachers, store owners, scientists, and pilots. Be sure to include children's own ideas on the chart, too.

 First Reading

Briefly review the title page and the table of contents, and then turn to pages 2 and 3. Have children point to the computer in each picture, and encourage them to read the text.

As children read, you might notice that they have trouble tracking multiple lines of text. Model how to use a ruler or a sheet of paper to help focus on one line at a time, moving the ruler or paper down to reveal the next line of text.

When children begin reading pages 9 through 13, make sure the recognize they repeated language pattern ___ *use computers.* Remind children that noticing repeated patterns in the text will help them read more fluently.

Rereading

Invite children to share parts of the book that seemed difficult, gently mentioning areas in the text where you observed the group struggling. Reread these passages, suggesting strategies or inviting children to offer their own strategy ideas. When children are able to read these pages more fluently, ask children to read the book again.

Discussing

Return to the two-column chart you created before reading that explored who uses computers and why. Compliment children on their ideas, pointing out those that were in the book. Then challenge children to think of other ways people might use computers. For example, have children ever used a computer in the library to find a library book? Have children ever seen cashiers in a grocery store using a computer? Elicit from children areas around the community where workers might use computers and for what purpose. Ask children what conclusions they can draw about computers; for example, "Computers are everywhere," or "Computers help people."

Teaching Points

Write the word *computer* on the board, and ask a volunteer to circle the ending letters *–er.* Then encourage children to look through the book for other words that end with *–er* or *–ers.* List the words children find on the board, and again ask children to circle the letters *–er* that they see.

Invite children to say the word *computer* with you and to clap the syllables. Make sure children are able to hear and clap the three syllables in *computer.* Say other words from the book at random, and ask children to repeat the words and clap along with the syllables again. Have children identify words with two syllables or three syllables, and sort the words in two columns on the board.

Reading and Writing Connections

Review with children the repeated language pattern ___ *use computers.* Have children copy the sentence and then come up with someone they know who uses a computer to complete it. Challenge children to write one or two more sentences to explain for what purpose the person uses the computer. Invite children to switch papers to read and share ideas.

School-to-Home Connection

Invite children to take home their School-to-Home book to read with their families. Ask children to talk with family members, family friends, and so on, to find out if and how they use computers for the work they do. Invite them to make a chart like the one made in class to organize their findings. Have them share their charts with the group.

Bibliography

Nonfiction

Cole, Joanna. (Adapted by Nancy White.) *Magic School Bus Gets Programmed: A Book About Computers, Vol. 1.* New York: Scholastic, Inc., 1999.

Kalman, Bobbie D. *Computer from A to Z.* New York: Crabtree Publishing Company, 1998.

Fiction

Brown, Marc. *Arthur's Computer Disaster.* Boston, MA: Little, Brown Children's Books, 1999.

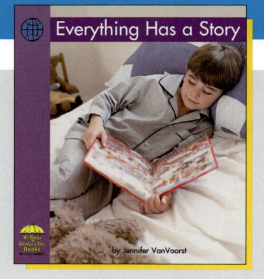

Everything Has a Story

by Jennifer VanVoorst

Standards and Benchmarks

See chart p. 88

Text Features

- **High-Frequency Words:** *a, all, an, and, are, at, be, been, came, can, did, do, done, has, have, in, it, its, of, off, on, or, said, so, some, that, the, their, them, they, to, too, up, us, was, we, with, you, your*
- **Phonics/Word Study:** digraph *th*, initial (*that, the, their, them, themselves, there, these, they, things, think*), medial (*everything, other, something*), final (*with*); long /a/ –ay (*may, play, way*); variant vowel /ô/ –all (*all, called, walls*), –ough (*bought, brought*); diphthong /ou/, spelled *ou* (*about*), *ow* (*down, how*); long /o/, spelled *ow* (*following, know, own*); /k/, spelled *ch* (*school*), *ck* (*picked*); /ô/ with *r*, spelled *or* (*orchard, stories*), *ore* (*store*); variant vowel /âr/ –are (*share*), –ear (*bear*), –ere (*there*); double consonants, medial (*called, following, happened, really*), final (*all, tell*)

Shared Reading

The Yellow Umbrella big books are designed to promote a shared reading experience that provides children with additional reading challenges while integrating and reinforcing content material from the student books. *Everything Has a Story* introduces children to history and storytelling and can be used to explore social studies content that includes the nature of community, personal histories, how objects came to be, and more. The text provides an opportunity for shared reading, but the book can be experienced without the text as well, as each photo can be used to explore multiple social studies concepts. In this way, *Everything Has a Story* serves as a concept resource that can be shared in new ways with each student book.

 Preparing for Reading

The night before you share the book with the class, choose an object that has a fun story behind it. The object should be simple, such as an old doll, an unusual hat, an inexpensive piece of jewelry, or a vacation souvenir. Show the item to the group, and tell children the story behind it. Preface your storytelling by saying, "This __ has a story." After the storytelling, invite children to look at objects around the room that have a story, such as a class project, a class pet, or a bulletin-board display. After children offer ideas, help them come up with a conclusion, and write the following sentence on the board: *Everything has a story.*

 Introducing the Book

Then present the book to the group, and challenge children to read the book title. Point out that the title matches the sentence you wrote on the board, and say it with the group. Looking at the cover, talk about which items children think might have a story. Then ask children to explain what "everything has a story" means. Record their ideas to review after reading.

 First Reading

Begin the book by exploring the title page. Have children read the book title with you, and read for them the author's name. Have them identify the table of contents, reviewing the purpose of the entries and page numbers. Mention that reading the table of contents can help them discover what they will read about.

Read pages 2 and 3 to the group, including the chapter title. Briefly let children talk about the idea of fictional stories versus true stories, and then continue reading. For this first reading of the big book, invite children to simply enjoy listening to you read; they do not need to read with you at this time. Explain that you would like them to enjoy the pictures and the words and to concentrate on the meaning of what you are reading. As you read, be sure to pronounce each word clearly and to pause at punctuation marks, modeling proper reading techniques. The benefit children will gain from this first reading is an example of good reading behavior, including fluency.

Rereading

Read the big book again, this time encouraging children to read along with you. Point to each word as you read to help children track print and follow along. Pause at difficult words and see if children are able to figure out and read the words on their own. Offer strategies for reading new words as needed.

Discussing

Have children repeat the title of the book, and ask if they think the title is true. Does everything have a story? To demonstrate the concept, pick up an ordinary object, like a piece of paper, and ask children what story it might have. (For example, how it was made from a tree or from recycled products.) Ask volunteers to choose an object from their desks and to imagine a story that the object might have. Let children have fun and be creative with their ideas. Also talk about whether their ideas are fictional or factual, and review the difference between made-up stories and true stories. As you make comparisons between the two, note ideas in a two-column chart.

Teaching Points

On the board, write verbs from the book that end with *–ed*, but only write the root word: *happen, call, pick*. Invite volunteers to make each word past tense by writing the letters *–ed* at the end.

Then write these verbs on the board: *grow, begin, send, make*. As children watch, add the letters *–ed* to the end of each, and say the words for the group. Ask children if these words sound

right: *growed, beginned, sended, maked*. Agree that these words do sound strange, and explain that the past tense is formed in a different way. In random order, write *grew, began, sent,* and *made*. Challenge children to match each word with its present tense. Work with children to write sentences for each word, too, both present and past tense.

Reading and Writing Connections

Give to partners an object about which to begin a story. Ask children to copy and complete this sentence with the object's name: *This ___ has a story.* Then tell children to brainstorm story ideas. Encourage them to consider such questions as, "How was it made? Where did it come from? Who owned it before? What does the object do all day?" Tell children to write down key words to express their ideas, and then have children record their stories into a tape recorder. Place the tape recorder and the object in your reading or story center for children to take turns enjoying each other's stories.

School-to-Home Connection

Ask children to look at home for a simple object to which a fun story is attached. Tell children to draw the object and then to write the story, asking for help from their families. Collect children's stories into a class book entitled, "The Stories We Can Tell!"

Bibliography

Nonfiction

Hindley, Judy. *A Piece of String Is a Wonderful Thing.* Cambridge, MA: Candlewick Press, 1995.

Marcos, Subcomandante. *The Story of Colors.* El Paso, TX: Cinco Puntos Press, 1999.

Powell, Patricia Hruby. *Blossom Tales: Flower Stories of Many Folk.* North Kingstown, RI: Moon Mountain Publishing, Inc., 2002.

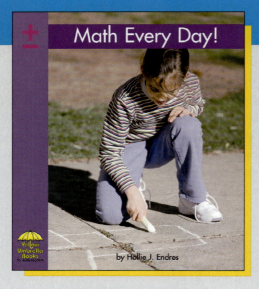

Math Every Day!

by Hollie J. Endres

Standards and Benchmarks

See chart p. 91

Text Features

- **High-Frequency Words:** *a, all, also, an, and, are, at, be, can, do, for, from, get, give, has, have, he, help, her, his, in, is, it, of, one, or, she, that, the, their, to, too, up, us, use, we, were, will, with, you, your*
- **Phonics/Word Study:** long /a/, spelled CVCe (*base-ball, cupcakes, games, lemonade, made, make, place,* *same, shapes, wake*), ay (*away, days, play, stay, ways*); long /i/, spelled CVCe (*decide, dimes, sides, time*); diphthong /ou/ (*around, count, house*); /k/, spelled *ck* (*clock*), *ch* (*school*); double consonants (*all, dessert, different, fall, glass, happen, selling*); /j/, spelled *j* (*jungle, subject*), *g* (*geography, gym*)

Shared Reading

The Yellow Umbrella big books are designed to promote a shared reading experience that provides children with additional reading challenges while integrating and reinforcing content material from the student books. *Math Every Day!* considers some of the many ways children use math in their daily lives and can be used to explore math concepts that include symmetry, money, adding, graphing, estimating, sorting, identifying and manipulating shapes, and more. The text provides an opportunity for shared reading, but the book can be experienced without the text as well, as each photo can be used to explore multiple math concepts. In this way, *Math Every Day!* serves as a concept resource that can be shared in new ways with each student book.

 ## Preparing for Reading

On the board, create a time line for the school day. Mark each segment as representing one hour or half hour. Then ask children to help you fill in the time line with the activities they do during the day. Encourage children to be specific, drawing from them activities for which they use math. For example, if they conducted a science experiment, have them explain any graphs or measurements. If you read aloud to them, note how many pages you read. For lunchtime, have children describe the amounts of foods they ate or drank. Review the time line, and ask children what they notice; they use math every day! Make sure they realize that the times on the time line are a way to use math, too.

 ## Introducing the Book

Display the book, and talk with children about all the ways they see math being used. Invite individual children to point to different math examples on the book cover. Organize children's ideas on the board in terms of the math principles being explored. Then ask children how they could summarize the book cover. What might be a good caption for this photograph? Help children read the book title, and then speculate with children which other "math moments" they might see in the book, jotting down their predictions.

 ## First Reading

Open the book to the title page, and have a volunteer point to the book title and author's name. Read both to the group. Then focus on the table of contents, and read the entries. Reread the first and last entries, and ask children what they can conclude. Confirm that the table of contents follows how math is used throughout the day. Ask, "What do you think we will read in the first chapter, 'Getting Ready'?"

Read the book out loud to the group, but do not encourage children to read along. As children listen to you read, they will hear a model of proper fluency, pronunciation, and phrasing, which will help them when they read on their own. Feel free to point to each word as you read it, but tell children to just listen to your voice and the words of the text.

Rereading

Now that children have heard the book once, turn to the beginning of the book, and invite children to read it with you. Again, point to each word as you read, encouraging children to follow along. You might drop out of the reading every few sentences, listening to the group read on their own. After each page, ask children to briefly summarize the math application you read about.

Discussing

Recall with children the math moments in the book. As you did before the reading, draw a time line on the board, and list children's responses in order from the beginning of the book to the end of the book, which loosely follows a day. Instead of hours for each time-line segment, write the chapter titles. Encourage children to help you complete the time line with ideas from the book, and then challenge them to come up with additional math moments, recalling specific times when they've used math. Incorporate children's ideas into the time line.

Teaching Points

Review with children the long /u/ sound in *school*. Write the word *school* on the board, and say it with the group. Invite a volunteer to circle the letters that make the long /u/ sound. Then have children replace the consonant cluster *sch* with another consonant to create a new word, such as *cool, pool, fool,* or *tool*. If children suggest words like *rule* or *mule*, write these words as well, pointing out the different spelling pattern. Continue with the long /u/ sound, using the phonograms *–ood* (*food, mood*) and *–oom* (*room, broom, gloom, bloom, doom, boom, zoom*).

Expand the lesson to include the variant vowel /oo/ sound, as in *wood*. Write *food* on the board, and then write *wood*. Say each word clearly so children can hear the different sounds made by the vowels. Then write other word pairs on

the board for children to say, such as *boot* and *foot, nook* and *noon, stood* and *stool,* and *cook* and *cool*.

Reading and Writing Connections

Invite children to contribute to a group big book about how they use math every day. Write the following sentence starters on the board: *I use math every day! When I ___ , I use math.* Give each child a large sheet of paper. The papers should be the same size. Have children copy and complete the sentence starter on the paper. Then ask them to illustrate their ideas. Combine the pages together, and then read the book back to the group.

School-to-Home Connection

Have children observe their family to find moments when they use math. It can be while following a recipe for dinner, playing a card or board game, or even checking times and channels while watching TV. Ask children to draw a "family portrait" that shows their families using math, and challenge them to write a caption, too. Then display children's work on a bulletin board titled "Math Every Day!"

Bibliography

Nonfiction

Amato, William. *Math at the Store.* New York: Scholastic, 2002. Also: *Math in the Back Yard* (2002), *Math in the Car* (2002), *Math in the Kitchen* (2002), *Math in the Neighborhood* (2002), *Math on the Playground* (2002).

Fiction

Crawford, Jean B. *Look Both Ways: City Math.* New York: Time Life, Inc., 1993.

Poetry

Hopkins, Lee Bennett. *Marvelous Math: A Book of Poems.* New York: Aladdin Paperbacks, 2001.

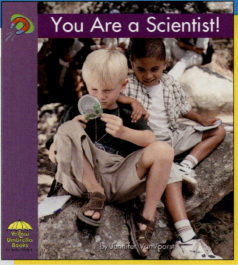

You Are a Scientist!

by Jennifer VanVoorst

Standards and Benchmarks

See chart p. 94

Text Features

- **High-Frequency Words:** *a, and, are, as, been, but, can, do, does, from, has, have, if, in, into, is, it, of, or, see, that, the, their, them, they, to, use, wants, will, you, your*
- **Phonics/Word Study:** diphthong /ou/, spelled *ou* (*about, around*), *ow* (*flowers, how*); word ending *–tion* (*attention, explanation, information, questions*); /ks/, spelled *x* (*explanation*); initial /w/, spelled *w* (*wants, way, ways, weight, wonder, work, world*), *wh* (*when, whether, why*); inflected word ending *–er* (*answer, gather, number, paper, whether, wonder*); short /i/ (*things, wings*); ending *y* (*discovery, family, many, study, sunny*); /sh/, spelled *sh* (*shadow, share, show*), *s* (*sure*); digraph *th*, initial (*that, the, their, them, they, things*), medial (*gather, something, whether*); silent *e* (*create, live, make, moles, notes, share, shines, solve, someone, something, sure, take, use*); variant vowel /ur/, spelled *or* (*work, world*), *–ear* (*learn*), *–ure* (*figure, sure*); variant vowel /är/ (*are, chart, far*); long /a/ *–eigh* (*weight*)

Shared Reading

The Yellow Umbrella big books are designed to promote a shared reading experience that provides children with additional reading challenges while integrating and reinforcing content material from the student books. *You Are a Scientist!* introduces children to the scientific method and serves as a springboard for further exploration of any science-related content. The text provides an opportunity for shared reading, but the book can be experienced without the text as well, as each photo can be used to explore multiple science concepts. In this way, *You Are a Scientist!* serves as a concept resource that can be shared in new ways with each student book.

 ### Preparing for Reading

Recite the following rhyming riddle to the group: "I like to look. I like to test. I ask questions. That's the best! I wonder 'how?' and 'what?' and 'why?' You are this. And so am I! What are we?" After children offer ideas, write the word *scientist* on the board. Challenge children to consider whether they think the last part of the riddle is correct—are they scientists, too? Let children freely exchange their ideas about scientists and the ways in which they, themselves, might be scientists.

 ### Introducing the Book

Present the book to the group, and have children respond to the cover. Ask children how the child on the cover is acting like a scientist, and help children identify the magnifying glass. Let children share experiences they have had with magnifying glasses or conducting experiments. Then direct their attention to the title. Encourage them to read the first three words on their own, then help them match the word *Scientist* with the word *scientist* you wrote on the board. Say the word for the group as you run your finger under the letters. Help them hear the syllable break between the letters *i* and *e*: Sci-en-tist.

 ### First Reading

Open the book, and explore with children the title page. After reading the title, talk about the picture. Then point to the author's name, and ask students if they know what these words tell the reader. Confirm that they name the book's author, and then read the name to them.

Preview the book by reading the table of contents to the group. Ask children what they notice about the entries, and point out that the entries are activities a scientist might do: asking questions, gathering information, making a guess, testing, learning, and sharing.

Turn to pages 2 and 3, and read the question posed in the chapter title. Then ask children what they notice about the first sentence—it is the same as the chapter title: *Who is a scientist?* Encourage children to briefly offer ideas about who is a scientist, and then continue reading pages 2 and 3.

For this first reading of the big book, invite children to listen to you read to them out loud. Point to each word as you read to help children follow along, but explain that they don't have to actually read with you. Instead, you would like them to focus on what the book is about and the sounds of the words and sentences as you read them. You might pause before you begin each page to let children make comments about the photograph. Suggest that they consider how the photograph relates to the text as you read the page to them.

 ## Rereading

Share with children some of the more difficult words you read. Tell children about the strategies you used silently to help you continue reading. Point out that even experienced readers often stumble over new words. Then return to the beginning of the book, and read it again. This time, encourage children to read aloud with you. Be sure to point to the words to guide the group.

 ## Discussing

Ask children if anything about the book surprised them. For example, were they surprised to learn that the simple act of asking questions about how things work—something they do quite often—is something that scientists do? Invite children to share some of the things they have wondered about and how they have tried to find answers.

 ## Teaching Points

Write words with the ending *–tion* on the board: *attention, explanation, information, question.*

Ask a volunteer to circle the letters that the words have in common. Point out that this spelling pattern makes its own unique sound, which is pronounced /shun/. Write other words on the board that end with *–tion*, but leave the ending blank. Ask children to come to the board to write in the missing letters. Point out that words that end with /shun/ are all nouns; for example: *nation, fiction, transportation, recreation, detention, creation.*

 ## Reading and Writing Connections

Tell children to write the following sentence at the top of a sheet of paper: *I am a scientist!* Then ask children to draw themselves doing something described in the book. Challenge children to write one or two more sentences that explain their pictures, and display children's work on a "We Are Scientists!" bulletin board.

 ## School-to-Home Connection

Tell children to interview one or two family members for ways in which they act like scientists. Encourage children to work with their families to write down the answers. Then have children share their answers with the group.

Bibliography

Nonfiction

Robinson, Tom Mark. *Everything Kids' Science Experiments Book.* Avon, MA: Adams Media Corporation, 2001.

St. George, Judith. *So You Want to Be an Inventor?* New York: Penguin Putnam Books for Young Readers, 2002.

Dorling Kindersley. *Science Kit.* New York: DK Publishing, 2002.

Book Title	Standards/Benchmarks National Social Studies Standards—National Council for the Social Studies Expectations of Excellence
All Kinds of Farms ▼ Set A	*Standard VII: Production, Distribution, and Consumption* d) give examples of the various institutions that make up economic systems such as families, workers, banks, labor unions, government agencies, small businesses, and large corporations; e) describe how we depend upon workers with specialized jobs and the ways in which they contribute to the production and exchange of goods and services.
At the Park	*Standard III: People, Places, and Environment* g) describe how people create places that reflect ideas, personality, culture, and wants and needs as they design homes, playgrounds, classrooms, and the like; h) examine the interaction of human beings and their physical environment, the use of land, building of cities, and ecosystem changes in selected locales and regions.
Everyone Eats Bread!	*Standard IV: Individual Development and Identity* a) explore and describe similarities and differences in the ways groups, societies, and cultures address similar human needs and concerns.
From Here to There	*Standard III: People, Places, and Environment* h) examine the interaction of human beings and their physical environment, the use of land, building of cities, and ecosystem changes in selected locales and regions.
What Does a Firefighter Do?	*Standard V: Individuals, Groups, and Institutions* g) show how groups and institutions work to meet individual needs and promote the common good, and identify examples of where they fail to do so. *Standard VI: Power, Authority, and Governance* c) give examples of how government does or does not provide for needs and wants of people, establish order and security, and manage conflict; d) recognize how groups and organizations encourage unity and deal with diversity to maintain order and security.
Working	*Standard VII: Production, Distribution, and Consumption* d) give examples of the various institutions that make up economic systems such as families, workers, banks, labor unions, government agencies, small businesses, and large corporations; e) describe how we depend upon workers with specialized jobs and the ways in which they contribute to the production and exchange of goods and services.

Celebrations

Standard I: Culture
a) explore and describe similarities and differences in the ways groups, societies, and cultures address similar human needs and concerns;
c) describe ways in which language, stories, folktales, music, and artistic creations serve as expressions of culture and influence behavior of people living in a particular culture;
e) give examples and describe the importance of cultural unity and diversity within and across groups.

Harvest Time

Standard III: People, Places, and Environments
h) examine the interaction of human beings and their physical environment, the use of land, building of cities, and ecosystem changes in selected locales and regions.
Standard VII: Production, Distribution, and Consumption
c) identify examples of private and public goods and services.

Homes

Standard I: Culture
a) explore and describe similarities and differences in the ways groups, societies, and cultures address similar human needs and concerns.
Standard III: People, Places, and Environments
g) describe how people create places that reflect ideas, personality, culture, and wants and needs as they design homes, playgrounds, classrooms, and the like;
h) examine the interaction of human beings and their physical environment, the use of land, building of cities, and ecosystem changes in selected locales and regions.

Making Money

Standard VII: Production, Distribution, and Consumption
a) give examples that show how scarcity and choice govern our economic decisions;
b) distinguish between needs and wants;
f) describe the influence of incentives, values, traditions, and habits on economic decisions;
g) explain and demonstrate the role of money in everyday life.

People Change the Land

Standard III: People, Places, and Environments
g) describe how people create places that reflect ideas, personality, culture, and wants and needs as they design homes, playgrounds, classrooms, and the like;
h) examine the interaction of human beings and their physical environment, the use of land, building of cities, and ecosystem changes in selected locales and regions.

Working Together

Standard IV: Individuals Development and Identity
h) work independently and cooperatively to accomplish goals.
Standard V: Individuals, Groups, and Institutions
a) identify roles as learned behavior patterns in group situations such as student, family member, peer play group member, or club member.
Standard IX: Global Connections
b) give examples of conflict, cooperation, and interdependence among individuals, groups, and nations.

Everything Has a Story

Standard II: Time, Continuity, and Change
b) demonstrate an ability to use correctly vocabulary associated with time such as *past*, *present*, *future*, and *long ago*; read and construct simple time lines; identify examples of change; and recognize examples of cause-and-effect relationships;
c) compare and contrast different stories or accounts about past events, people, places, or situations, identifying how they contribute to our understanding of the past.

Math

Book Title

Standards/Benchmarks
National Math Standards—National Council of Teachers of Mathematics

Set A

Adding Arctic Animals

Numbers and Operations Standard for PreK-2
Understand meanings of operations and how they relate to one another:
- understand various meanings of addition and subtraction of whole numbers and the relationship between the two operations;
- understand the effects of adding and subtracting whole numbers.
Compute fluently and make reasonable estimates:
- develop and use strategies for whole-number computations, with a focus on addition and subtraction;
- develop fluency with basic number combinations for addition and subtraction.

Algebra Standard for PreK-2
Use mathematical models to represent and understand quantitative relationships:
- model situations that involve the addition and subtraction of whole numbers, using objects, pictures, and symbols.

Animal Patterns

Algebra Standard for PreK-2
Understand patterns, relations, and functions:
- recognize, describe, and extend patterns such as sequences of sounds and shapes or simple numeric patterns and translate from one representation to another;
- analyze how both repeating and growing patterns are generated.

City Shapes

Geometry Standard for PreK-2
Analyze characteristics and properties of two- and three-dimensional geometric shapes and develop mathematical arguments about geometric shapes:
- recognize, name, build, draw, compare, and sort two- and three-dimensional shapes;
- describe attributes and parts of two- and three-dimensional shapes;
- investigate and predict the results of putting together and taking

apart two- and three-dimensional shapes.

Use visualization, spatial reasoning, and geometric modeling to solve problems:
- create mental images of geometric shapes using spatial memory and spatial visualization;
- recognize and represent shapes from different perspectives;
- relate ideas in geometry to ideas in number and measurement;
- recognize geometric shapes and structures in the environment and specify their location.

Count Your Chickens	*Number and Operations Standard for Grades PreK-2* Understand numbers, ways of representing numbers, relationships among numbers, and number systems: • develop understanding of the relative position and magnitude of whole numbers and of ordinal and cardinal numbers and their connections; • develop a sense of whole numbers and represent and use them in flexible ways, including relating, composing, and decomposing numbers; • connect number words and numerals to the quantities they represent, using various physical models and representations.
It's Time	*Measurement Standard for Grades PreK-2* Understand measurable attributes of objects and the units, systems, and processes of measurement: • recognize the attributes of length, volume, weight, area, and time; • compare and order objects according to these attributes; • select an appropriate unit and tool for the attribute being measured. Apply appropriate techniques, tools, and formulas to determine measurements: • use tools to measure; • develop common referents for measures to make comparisons and estimates.
One Green Frog	*Numbers and Operations Standard for PreK-2* Understand numbers, ways of representing numbers, relationships among numbers, and number systems: • count with understanding and recognize "how many" in sets of objects; • develop understanding of the relative position and magnitude of whole numbers and of ordinal numbers and cardinal numbers and their connections; • develop a sense of whole numbers and represent and use them in flexible ways, including relating, composing, and decomposing numbers; • connect number words and numerals to the quantities they represent, using various physical models and representations.

Can You Guess?

Set B

Number and Operations Standard for Grades PreK-2
Compute fluently and make reasonable estimates:
- use a variety of methods and tools to compute, including objects, mental computation, estimation, paper and pencil, and calculators.

Measurement Standard for Grades PreK-2
Understand measurable attributes of objects and the units, systems, and processes of measurement:
- recognize the attributes of length, volume, weight, area, and time;
- compare and order objects according to these attributes.

Apply appropriate techniques, tools, and formulas to determine measurements:
- develop common referents for measures to make comparisons and estimates.

Let's Graph

Data Analysis and Probability for Grades PreK-2
Formulate questions that can be addressed with data and collect, organize, and display relevant data to answer them:
- pose questions and gather data about themselves and their surroundings;
- sort and classify objects according to their attributes and organize data about the objects;
- represent data using concrete objects, pictures, and graphs.

Select and use appropriate statistical methods to analyze data:
- describe parts of the data and the set of data as a whole to determine what the data show.

Develop and evaluate inferences and predictions that are based on data:
- discuss events related to students' experiences as likely or unlikely.

Look at Both Sides

Geometry Standards for Grades PreK-2
Apply transformations and use symmetry to analyze mathematical situations:
- recognize and apply slides, flips, and turns;
- recognize and create shapes that have symmetry.

Making Shapes

Geometry Standard for PreK-2
Analyze characteristics and properties of two- and three-dimensional geometric shapes and develop mathematical arguments about geometric shapes:
- recognize, name, build, draw, compare, and sort two- and three-dimensional shapes;
- describe attributes and parts of two- and three-dimensional shapes;
- investigate and predict the results of putting together and taking apart two- and three-dimensional shapes.

Use visualization, spatial reasoning, and geometric modeling to solve problems:
- create mental images of geometric shapes using spatial memory and spatial visualization;
- recognize and represent shapes from different perspectives;
- relate ideas in geometry to ideas in number and measurement;
- recognize geometric shapes and structures in the environment and specify their location.

Money Math	*Number and Operations Standard for Grades PreK-2* Understand numbers, ways of representing numbers, relationships among numbers, and number systems: • count with understanding and recognize "how many" in sets of objects; • use multiple models to develop initial understandings of place value and the base-ten number system; connect number words and numerals to the quantities they represent, using various physical models and representations. Understand meanings of operations and how they relate to one another: • understand various meanings of addition and subtraction of whole numbers and the relationship between the two operations; • understand situations that entail multiplication and division, such as equal groupings of objects and sharing equally.
Parts of a Whole	*Number and Operations Standard for Grades PreK-2* Understand numbers, ways of representing numbers, relationships among numbers, and number systems: • understand and represent commonly used fractions, such as 1/4, 1/3, and 1/2; • connect number words and numerals to the quantities they represent, using various physical models and representations.
Math Every Day! Big Book	*Problem Solving Standard for Grades PreK-2* Instructional programs from prekindergarten through grade 12 should enable all students to: • build new mathematical knowledge through problem solving; • solve problems that arise in mathematics and in other contexts; • apply and adapt a variety of appropriate strategies to solve problems; • monitor and reflect on the process of mathematical problem solving. *Communication Standard for Grades PreK-2* Instructional programs from prekindergarten through grade 12 should enable all students to: • organize and consolidate their mathematical thinking through communication; • communicate their mathematical thinking coherently and clearly to peers, teachers, and others; • analyze and evaluate the mathematical thinking and strategies of others; • use the language of mathematics to express mathematical ideas precisely.

Book Title	Standards/Benchmarks
	Benchmarks for Science Literacy: Project 2061

Mammals — Set A

Standard 5A: The Living Environment—Diversity of Life (K-2)
- Some animals and plants are alike in the way they look and in the things they do, and others are very different from one another.
- Plants and animals have features that help them live in different environments.

Standard 5B: The Living Environment—Heredity (K-2)
- There is a variation among individuals of one kind within a population.

The Ocean

Standard 5D: The Living Environment—Interdependence of Life (K-2)
- Living things are found almost everywhere in the world. There are somewhat different kinds in different places.

Standard 5F: The Living Environment—Evolution of Life (K-2)
- Different plants and animals have external features that help them thrive in different kinds of places.

Push and Pull

Standard 4F: The Physical Setting—Motion (K-2)
- The way to change how something is moving is to give it a push or a pull.

Show Us Your Wings

Standard 5A: The Living Environment—Diversity of Life (K-2)
- Some animals and plants are alike in the way they look and in the things they do, and others are very different from one another.
- Plants and animals have features that help them live in different environments.

Standard 5B: The Living Environment—Heredity (K-2)
- There is a variation among individuals of one kind within a population.

Trees Are Terrific!

Standard 5A: The Living Environment—Diversity of Life (K-2)
- Some animals and plants are alike in the way they look and in the things they do, and others are very different from one another.
- Plants and animals have features that help them live in different environments.

Standard 5F: The Living Environment—Evolution of Life (K-2)
- Different plants and animals have external features that help them thrive in different kinds of places.

Who Builds?

Standard 4C: The Physical Setting—Processes that Shape the Earth (K-2)
- Animals and plants sometimes cause changes in their surroundings.

Standard 8B: The Designed World—Materials and Manufacturing (K-2)
- Some kinds of materials are better than others for making any particular thing. Materials that are better in some ways (such as stronger or cheaper) may be worse in other ways (heavier or harder to cut).

Eating Well Set B	*Standard 6E: The Human Organism—Physical Health (K-2)* • Eating a variety of healthful foods and getting enough exercise and rest help people to stay healthy. • Some things people take into their bodies from the environment can hurt them.
Everything Is Matter!	*Standard 4D: The Physical Setting—Structure of Matter (K-2)* • Objects can be described in terms of the materials they are made of (clay, cloth, paper, etc.) and their physical properties (color, size, shape, weight, texture, flexibility, etc.). • Things can be done to materials to change some of their properties, but not all materials respond the same way to what is done to them.
Let's Look at Rocks	*Standard 4C: The Physical Setting—Processes that Shape the Earth (K-2)* • Chunks of rocks come in many sizes and shapes, from boulders to grains of sand and even smaller.
Make It Move!	*Standard 4F: The Physical Setting—Motion (K-2)* • Things move in many different ways, such as straight, zigzag, around and around, back and forth, and fast and slow. *Standard 6A: The Human Organism—Human Identity (3-5)* • Human beings have made tools and machines to sense and do things that they could not otherwise sense or do at all, or as quickly, or as well.
Snakes and Lizards	*Standard 5A: The Living Environment—Diversity of Life (K-2)* • Some animals and plants are alike in the way they look and in the things they do, and others are very different from one another. • Plants and animals have features that help them live in different environments. *Standard 5B: The Living Environment—Heredity (K-2)* • There is a variation among individuals of one kind within a population.
What Computers Do	*Standard 8D: The Designed World—Communication (K-2)* • Devices can be used to send and receive messages quickly and clearly. *Standard 8E: The Designed World—Information Processing (K-2)* • There are different ways to store things so they can be easily found later.

You Are a Scientist!

Standard 1B: The Nature of Science—Scientific Inquiry (K-2)
- People can often learn about things around them by just observing those things carefully, but sometimes they can learn more by doing something to the things and noting what happens.
- Tools such as thermometers, magnifiers, rulers, or balances often give more information about things than can be obtained by just observing things without their help.
- Describing things as accurately as possible is important in science because it enables people to compare their observations with those of others.

Standard 1C: The Nature of Science—The Scientific Enterprise (K-2)
- Everybody can do science and invent things and ideas.
- In doing science, it is often helpful to work with a team and to share findings with others. All team members should reach their own individual conclusions, however, about what the findings mean.
- A lot can be learned about plants and animals by observing them closely, but care must be taken to know the needs of living things and how to provide for them in the classroom.

Name _____   Date _____

Have children briefly answer the following.
Children may dictate to you or write their own answers.

_____
Title of the book

_____
Something I learned from the book

_____
The page number of my favorite picture from the book

_____
A difficult word from the book

A drawing of how this book connects to me

Student Record

Name _____ Date _____

Book Title _____ Level _____

Reading Behaviors and Strategies to Note	Consistently	Sometimes	Not Yet	Notes
Enjoys reading books				
Remembers facts from text				
Uses picture cues to comprehend text				
Recognizes many high-frequency words and reads them automatically				
Uses decoding skills for difficult or unfamiliar vocabulary				
Rereads text for comprehension				
Self-monitors comprehension by asking questions				
Makes and confirms predictions				
Engages background knowledge and prior experiences during reading				
Reads aloud with fluency				
Chooses to read books from different genrés on different topics				